MANAGING NARCISSISTS, BLAMERS, DRAMATICS AND MORE...

Research-Driven Scripts For Managing Difficult Personalities At Work

Mark Murphy

Founder of Leadership IQ

978-1-7320484-6-1 Paperback
978-1-7320484-7-8 Ebook

To Andrea, Isabella, and Andrew

FOR MORE INFORMATION

For free downloadable resources including quizzes and discussion guides, please visit www.leadershipiq.com

TABLE OF CONTENTS

INTRODUCTION

Managing difficult personalities is never fun. Most of these tough-to-manage people have had years of practice at behaving badly and very few of them have any desire to change. That's why it takes a targeted, scientific approach to make an impact.

This book shows you how to motivate the difficult personalities in your workplace to become more productive and pleasant to be around. You'll learn how to dial back their negativity and to put a stop to the drama, confusion, chaos and conflict that makes them so problematic.

Difficult personalities aren't just annoying, frustrating and exhausting; in many cases they directly diminish (and even destroy) business value because they wield real power over other team members. And when those other team members find difficult personalities intimidating, demoralizing and fatiguing, you're going to see higher turnover, lost productivity, breakdowns and miscommunication, and much more.

Good people don't want to work with low performers who divert the boss's time and attention, slow down productivity, and who turn work into an emotionally difficult environment. When we conducted a survey of more than 70,000 employees, one question we asked was "What's it like to work with folks who have a lousy attitude?" 87% said coworkers with poor attitudes make them so miserable that they have seriously considered changing jobs. Even worse, 93% admitted their productivity level dropped when forced to work alongside coworkers with poor attitudes.

The emotional antics and behavioral distractions displayed by difficult personalities destroy the positive flow of work. According to Leadership IQ's study "Interruptions at Work Are Killing Your Productivity," 71% of people report frequent interruptions at work and only 29% report being able to block out those interruptions in order to focus on their work.[i]

There's also the issue of time. Research shows that shaping an optimally motivated, engaged, inspired, and innovative team requires that a boss or manager spend around six hours per week interacting with employees. In fact, employees who spend six hours with their boss or manager are 29% more inspired—30% more engaged—and 16% more innovative than people who only spend one hour per week interacting with their leader.[ii]

Spending time with your best people should be a priority, but 93% of leaders surveyed said they spend significantly more time with low performers, and that includes difficult personalities. What's more, the time spent with difficult personalities sends a clear message to high performers about where you place your priorities. And when the bulk of your time goes to solving problems created by difficult personalities, it leaves your good people without the leadership they want and need.

Even more disturbing is that difficult personalities are often happier at work than are the good people who work for you. When Leadership IQ matched engagement survey and performance appraisal data for 207 organizations, in 42% of the organizations studied, low performers were MORE engaged than high and middle performers.[iii] And one big reason why so many high performers are disengaged is the burn out they feel from working alongside low performers including Dramatics, Blamers, the Confidently Incompetent, Overly Sensitives and more.

Finally, you owe it to yourself to learn how to effectively manage difficult personalities. Unfortunately, too many leaders neglect to consider this until it's too late, but when you allow these low performing employees to persist, they will wreck your reputation as a leader and can even cost you your job.

Our four-year study "Why CEOs Get Fired" concluded that tolerating low performers accounts for 27% of CEO firings.[iv] Allowing attitudinal low performers, including Negative Personalities, Problem Bringers, Advantage Takers, Narcissists, Talented Terrors and more to exist in the workplace can destroy a leader's reputation and make it politically difficult to hold other employees accountable to expected behavioral standards.

This book introduces simple behavioral management techniques for stopping the bad behaviors that make difficult personalities so difficult. You'll learn to use tools including redirection, reframing, and fact-focused dialogue to get good results without being confrontational.

Confronting a difficult personality with admonishments such as "You know that's not true" or "Stop being so dramatic" or "Toughen up" or "Why are you so darn sensitive to everything I say," may feel tempting. But confrontation only makes difficult personalities even more difficult to manage. Most of these people want to suck you into their emotional vortex, and when they succeed in making you lose your cool, it only empowers them more.

The good news is that we're not going to play their game (because their game is messy, emotionally draining and time-consuming). Instead, we're going to use a calm, quiet and non-confrontational approach to managing difficult personalities, and that's what this book provides. Even managers who feel a bit intimidated by difficult personalities can use these techniques to great effect.

The following chapters address nine of the most common difficult personalities found in the workplace. We'll cover Dramatics, Negative Personalities, Blamers, Problem Bringers, Overly Sensitives,

Advantage-Takers, the Confidently Incompetent, Narcissists and Talented Terrors (people who are highly skilled but have a lousy attitude). Each chapter introduces a new difficult personality, shares valuable research, and teaches the correct behavioral management approach (including scripts) so you know exactly what to do and say to make real change. Each chapter also includes real-life examples shared by managers who have successfully used these techniques to manage the difficult personalities in their workplaces.

I do have a few words of caution before we begin. Difficult personalities are nearly always distracting and disruptive. However, should any difficult personality move into exhibiting behaviors that are potentially dangerous, it's critical to immediately consult your human resources department, your legal department, your security department, or whatever resources you have in place to handle potentially dangerous situations.

Now, let's get started.

CHAPTER 1

SHIFT YOUR MINDSET TO MANAGE DIFFICULT PERSONALITIES

You're about to learn science-backed techniques and scripts for radically changing someone else's difficult behaviors. These tactics are not difficult to use, but there are certain mindsets that can either hinder or help you in achieving best results.

So before we get into the tools and scripts you'll use to manage difficult personalities, let's look at seven key mental shifts that you may need to make.

Mindset Shift #1: We Need to Think and Speak Factually (With the FIRE Model)

A lot of the difficult personalities we manage are swirling maelstroms of negative emotions and misinterpretations. While some may masquerade as aloof and hyper-analytical, most difficult personalities infect our team with hurt feelings, irrational assumptions, and the like. To counter the emotional turbulence of difficult personalities, we need to be as factual, unemotional and rational as possible.

This is easier to understand when we use a tool called the FIRE Model (Figure 1.1). FIRE stands for **Facts, Interpretations, Reactions** and desired **Ends**, and these four pieces explain the essential way that we humans typically evaluate the world around us.

- First, we notice some **Facts**.
- Second, we make **Interpretations** about those facts.
- Third, based on our interpretations, we experience emotional **Reactions**.
- Fourth, once we experience those emotions, we have some desired **Ends**.

Facts are observable and objective reality; you can videotape, transcribe or otherwise document and measure the facts. The facts are also unemotional. But the way most of us process information is we see a fact (or a set of facts) and we then make an interpretation of that fact. An interpretation is where we give the facts some extra meaning.

The human brain is essentially an interpretation machine, which explains why people can have such differing perceptions

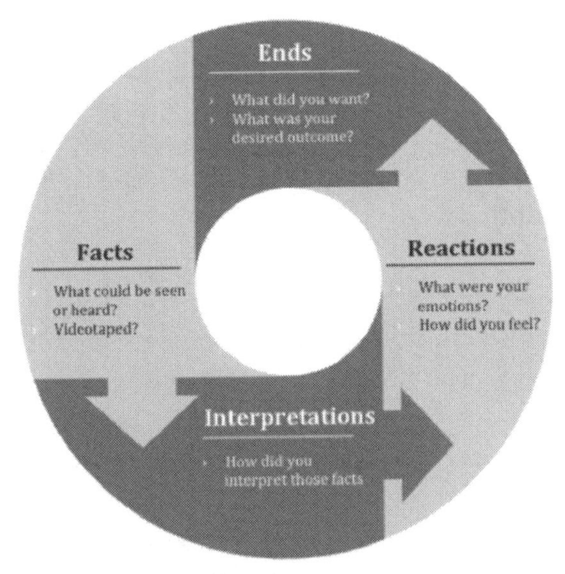

Figure 1.1 Fire Model.

(sometimes radically so) of this world we all share. The brain doesn't show us the world as it factually is, but rather, when we observe a fact, the brain almost instantaneously sifts through our unique personal past experiences and accumulated knowledge to assign meaning, or intent, to that fact. This is an interpretation, and while sometimes it works in our favor, there are times when it works against us.

Imagine that it's nighttime and you're about to fall asleep when you hear a rustling in the bushes outside your bedroom window. You don't unemotionally think, "Hmm, a rustling in the bushes. I am noting the existence of those sound waves." Instead, your brain goes to work trying to assign some meaning to that rustling in the bushes by referencing your life experiences and your history with similar situations. For example, your interpretation of the fact that there's a rustling in the bushes might be that it's just the neighbor's dog sniffing around your yard again. But your interpretation could also be that something awful is coming to attack you. It all depends on how your brain interprets the facts.

In the workplace, we might observe the fact that Bob spoke up four times in this morning's meeting. Based on this fact, our brains might make the interpretation that Bob is doing a good job and he's got some interesting ideas to share. According to the FIRE Model, once the brain leaps from facts to interpretations, we next have an emotional reaction. So if we've made a positive interpretation that Bob had some interesting ideas in the meeting, our emotional reaction might be "I'm feeling good about Bob and the value he brings to the company."

Once we have that emotional reaction, we're then going to have some desired end. We've gone from fact to interpretation to emotional reaction, and now we want something to happen. Based on our positive emotional reaction about Bob, that desired end might be "I'm going to ask Bob to join the product discovery team." In this case, while we moved within milliseconds from facts to interpretations to reactions and ends, the net effect was pretty positive (i.e. Bob spoke up in the morning meeting and now he's on the product discovery team).

For difficult personalities, of course, that flow from fact to interpretation to emotional reaction to desired ends will look quite a bit different. When Bob spoke up four times in this morning's meeting, a difficult personality might make the interpretation that "Bob is trying to make me look stupid by hogging all the time in the meeting." That could lead to an intensely negative emotional reaction (e.g. "I hate Bob so much"), which, in turn, could drive the difficult personality to sabotage Bob's next project (i.e. their desired end).

Whether our personality is built on sunshine and rainbows, or gloom and darkness, we humans typically evaluate the world through the FIRE Model. We observe a **Fact**, we make an **Interpretation** about that fact, we then have an emotional **Reaction** which leads to a desired **End**.

Once we understand this model, we can use it to keep ourselves focused on thinking and speaking factually (especially when addressing difficult personalities). The more we remain rooted in the world of facts, the calmer and smarter we'll be. And the more our conversations with difficult personalities are focused on facts, the more likely they are to receive our message.

Imagine that an employee storms into your office and exclaims, "I'm so hurt and upset that you feel that I'm too dramatic!" There are emotions and interpretations embedded in that sentence, and all those 'feeling words' show that this person is thinking neither factually nor calmly. If we respond with emotions, even if we say something nice like "I feel bad that you're upset," we're keeping this person in an emotionally charged state.

If we want this person to process our feedback and to respond by consciously altering their behavior, we need them less (and not more) emotionally charged. Avoiding emotional language and speaking factually helps to guide people towards more analytical and logical ways of thinking.

For starters, this means not saying the F-Word, and by this, I mean "feel" (e.g. "I *feel* bad that you're upset."). Thinking and speaking factually also means avoiding words like *always, never, forever, impossible,* and *constantly*. If we say, "You're always negative," or "You never take responsibility," or "You're constantly taking credit for others' work," we're not being factual. Absolute statements that indicate something is one hundred percent one way or another are only true when there's not one single instance where it was otherwise. So if you tell someone "You're always negative" but they can point to that one time, and it could be 20 years ago, when they did something positive, it proves your statement false.

Thinking and speaking factually requires avoiding inflammatory and accusatory language that stirs up emotions. When we keep our thoughts and words factual, we're keeping ourselves relatively calm. That, in turn, helps to keep our difficult personalities calm so they can better process our request for behavioral change.

Mindset Shift #2: We're Doing Behavior Management, Not Therapy

When managing difficult personalities, we're not trying to "fix" their underlying personality issues. It would be great if that were possible, but therapeutically addressing the underlying issues that drive difficult personalities is a deeply complicated and difficult job.

I know this can be tough news to hear. Good leaders typically have a knack for coaching people along with a positive 'can-do' attitude and a love of big challenges. And experience tells me that the more I say, "You can't truly fix a difficult personality," the more this will motivate certain leaders to want to prove me wrong.

"Can't" may not be an easy word to hear, but in this case, it absolutely applies.

Most of these difficult personalities don't want to be "fixed." They didn't seek you out for counseling because they felt a dissatisfaction with the current state of their life. In fact, the opposite is typically true. Difficult personalities have been enabled and coddled for years and thus feel absolutely no impetus to change their difficult behavior. And despite how obvious it is to everyone else; many difficult personalities lack any awareness of how problematic their bad attitudes and behaviors actually are.

It's the rare leader who has either the resources or the required professional training to "fix" a difficult personality. There's also the matter of time. Consider all the people who need your time and attention. Every extra hour you spend trying to address the underlying issues afflicting difficult personalities is an hour you take away from your good employees, customers, and colleagues. You have a choice: you can give your time to the people who want and deserve it (e.g. customers, high performers, etc.), or you can give your time to the people who will fight you every step of the way (i.e. difficult personalities).

Bottom line, we're not going to try and change the person. Our goal here is much easier, and it's something that anyone can do. We're simply going to stop the bad behaviors that make difficult personalities so difficult.

Mindset Shift #3: Our Only Goal Is Behavioral Change

As a corollary to Mindset Shift #2 above, our only goal in managing difficult personalities is to effect behavioral change. It doesn't matter if difficult employees apologize for, or feel bad about, their difficult behaviors. All that truly matters is getting them to change those difficult behaviors.

Imagine that you've got an overly dramatic employee who, after a deep conversation with you, apologizes profusely for their history of dramatic behavior. But then, at a meeting five days later, that person is back to causing a ruckus with their drama and histrionics. Is that really what you want? Wouldn't you rather have someone who didn't apologize but who did quietly alter their dramatic behavior?

It's natural to place a high value on apologies. Most of us learned about the value of the apology very early in life, often from parents who admonished us with some form of "you're not leaving this room until you apologize." There's even a virtual industry built on pundits analyzing the sincerity of the apologies made by politicians, athletes and anyone remotely famous. But when it comes to managing difficult personalities, we must make a choice: we can direct our conversations towards extracting an apology or towards effecting behavioral change.

Coercing an apology out of a difficult personality might feel momentarily mollifying, but the chances are slim that anything about that person's behavior will change. Our goal must be behavioral change. If we happen to get a truly sincere apology, that's great, but it shouldn't be the primary goal.

Mindset Shift #4: Tackle Issues as Quickly as Possible

We've all heard that the most effective time to give feedback to an employee is right away; the closer the feedback is to the actual poor behavior, the easier it is for the employee to make a mental connection between the two.

But there's another very important (and slightly selfish) reason why we should tackle issues as quickly as possible. One of the challenges with difficult personalities is that the things they say and do often stick in our craws for days, weeks, or even years. We just can't let it go. I'm willing to bet that you've gone home after a trying day of dealing with a difficult personality and spent the evening replaying an especially frustrating conversation with that employee in your head.

Most leaders experience this, but the more we ruminate about these difficult employees, the angrier and more frustrated it makes us. And the angrier we feel, the less calm, cool and analytical we're going to be when we take steps to manage them.

Some difficult employees will test the limits of our intellect and our emotional control. This means that we need to be on our A game to successfully navigate these conversations. But when there's frustration or resentment lurking in the back of our minds, we're mentally compromised, and relatively minor issues can spark a major blow-up.

Don't let your frustrations build. When you see blame, drama, negativity, etc., tackle it right away. One of the benefits of this book is that it gives you a toolkit of phrases you can use on-the-fly. There's no need to wait days, let alone weeks or months, to address these issues. And believe me, life is infinitely better when you no longer take home with you the irritations and annoyances of dealing with difficult personalities.

Mindset Shift #5: You Will Probably Need to Tone Down Your Empathy

It's become cliché to assert that having high emotional intelligence, of which empathy is an important facet, equals better performance for leaders. But I'm going to shock you, because the link between emotional intelligence and job performance is wildly overstated, especially when we're managing difficult personalities.

The research shows that in certain jobs, having higher emotional intelligence is correlated with lower job performance. In 2010, researchers at the University of Illinois at Urbana-Champaign conducted an exhaustive meta-analysis of every available study linking emotional intelligence to job performance. They analyzed 476 such studies, involving 191 distinct jobs, and concluded that the determining factor in whether emotional intelligence would be positively or negatively related to job performance was something called "emotional labor."[v]

Emotional labor is the extent to which we must regulate and display certain emotions to achieve our goals. For example, nursing is a job with high emotional labor; it involves lots of empathy, expressing positive emotions, etc. By contrast, low emotional labor jobs, like some accountants, welders, and programmers, have less need for showing lots of empathy.

The research discovered that in jobs with high emotional labor, like nursing, having high levels of emotional intelligence and empathy led to better job performance. That's intuitive. But in jobs with low emotional labor, like some accountants, welders, and programmers, having high empathy led to lower job performance!

In general, empathy (understanding and sharing the feelings of others) is a great thing. But imagine you're a commission-driven cold-calling salesperson. The job dictates that every day you face rejection, insults and objections, so a key to your financial and psychological survival is the thickness of your skin. You might need to withstand 50 angrily disconnected calls and still make the 51st call undaunted.

If you empathize too much with each person on your calling list, you might start to question the very nature of your job. For example, you might think: "Am I really annoying when I call?" or "Maybe I shouldn't interrupt people while they're working," or "I guess that I wouldn't like getting these calls either."

In general, having high levels of empathy and emotional intelligence is fantastic for leadership. But when it comes to managing difficult personalities, our job is much like the cold-calling salesperson who requires an incredibly thick skin. In other words, too much empathy is going to impede our ability to manage difficult personalities.

I know that many of my readers are incredibly nice, caring, empathic leaders, and I would never want that to change. But in the case of managing difficult personalities, you must remain calm, cool, and even a bit aloof. Many difficult personalities are masters at manipulation; they know how to tug at heart strings, and they excel at derailing conversations and inflaming emotions. We can only be fully successful in counteracting that by keeping some emotional distance and by dialing down some of our empathy.

Mindset Shift #6: We Need to Stop Characterizing Difficult Personalities as 'High Performers with Difficult Attitudes'

Not all difficult personalities are alike. It might be a Narcissist that's upsetting your workplace, or a Blamer, or a Dramatic, or someone else. Each type of difficult personality plays out through different behaviors. That's why we need a unique approach for managing each type of difficult personality.

But there is one trait that many difficult personalities do share, and it's that these employees, while difficult and frustrating, typically aren't all bad. Most of them bring some level of skill to the job, because if they didn't (if they had a bad attitude and poor skills), it would have been easy to fire them by now.

Skill is one of the things that makes it so challenging to hold difficult personalities accountable for their disruptive attitudes and behaviors. They've got some talent and they can prove it, and that gives them a platform from which to fight back when receiving critical feedback (e.g. "How dare you tell me I'm overly dramatic when you know I'm the best person on the team").

Most managers admit that managing an employee with a difficult personality is tough, but when that employee has skills, they stop short at labeling them a low performer. Too many managers will mistakenly say "You mean Frank in accounting? I'll admit; he doesn't do anything without an argument first, but that's just who he is. Besides, he's got talent. He may have a lousy attitude, but he's still got what it takes to be a high performer."

Classifying a difficult personality as a high performer, even a 'high performer with a difficult personality,' is a dangerous mistake. If you want to manage these employees effectively, then you must accept that there's no such thing as a high performer with a lousy attitude. As long as their bad behaviors persist, they are low performers. And if you don't address them as such, you're putting the organization, your team, and your job at risk. And there's substantial study to back this.

In preparing to write my book, *Hiring For Attitude*, my team and I conducted a three-year hiring study that tracked 5,000 leaders who collectively hired over 20,000 employees.[vi] The results of this study are significant to every facet of leadership; not just hiring.

For instance, we learned that 46% of new hires fail within 18 months of starting the job. That's unsettling to hear, but here's the part that's really critical: out of the 46% of employees who fail to become any kind of acceptable performer, let alone a high performer, only 11% of the time a lack of technical ability, or skill, is to blame. 89% of the time a lousy attitude is the clear reason behind employee failure.

Our study also identified the top attitudinal issues that bring new hires down:

- 26% fail due to lack of Coachability. These people don't accept and implement feedback from bosses, colleagues, customers and others.
- 23% fail due to poor emotional intelligence. These people lack the ability to understand and manage their own emotions and to accurately assess others' emotions.
- 17% fail due to lack of motivation. These people lack the positive attitudes that fuel the drive to achieve their full potential and to excel at the job.

- 15% fail due to the wrong temperament. These people have the wrong attitude and personality for a particular job and work environment.

All nine of the difficult personalities covered in this book fall into at least one of those four problematic attitudinal categories. And while this information should certainly make you rethink how you hire, it also shows that no matter how skilled someone is, if they also have a bad attitude, that person is a low performer.

If your organization is like most, you may be allowing your difficult personalities to go unchecked. Consider, for example, the company standards used to evaluate employee performance. Most leaders still depend upon skill-based criteria, even though we now know that aptitude factors such as knowledge of work and the quantity and quality of that work are only responsible for 11% of employee failure.

Even performance reviews that incorporate an attitude assessment (and most don't) can fail to identify difficult personalities. That's because high skills ratings create a halo effect that distorts the truth about a lousy attitude. A Narcissist can be making your life a total nightmare, but if they are getting 5 out of 5 on their performance review due to their great skills, you're actually rewarding them for their difficult attitude—in spite of all the damage they do.

Holding difficult personalities accountable for their bad behavior requires adopting a mindset that recognizes these employees as low performers. Remember that when the best people on your team find difficult personalities intimidating, demoralizing and fatiguing, you're going to see higher turnover, lost productivity, breakdowns and miscommunication, and much more. It might not always seem like Narcissists, Blamers, Dramatics, etc. require the low performer label, but because their difficult personalities ultimately erode business value, it's the label that fits best.

Mindset Shift #7: Say "Thank You" To Your High and Middle Performers

One way to increase your odds of successfully managing low performing difficult personalities is to first give a little extra love to your high and middle performers.

You've got high performers and you've got middle performers; employees who show up every day, who are successful in their work, and who don't drive everyone crazy with their difficult personalities. From time to time, it's a good idea to boost your relationship with these good people, and increase their motivation, by calling them into your office just to say, "thank you."

This isn't meaningless praise. You're going to specifically thank these good employees for a couple of the best things that they've recently done. These should be performance aspects that you want to reinforce and that you'd like to see even more of.

For example, you might say, "Bob, thank you. I probably don't say this often enough, but specifically, I want to say thank you for the way you got the Johnson account report done 13 days ahead of schedule. It really made a difference to the client and they're going to give us their next big contract." Or, you might say, "Thank you, Pat, for working all day Saturday to finish the big report," or "Thank you, Sally, for the way you put those extra data analyses at the front of the report that we delivered to ACME Corp. They thought that was the best proposal they've ever received."

Whatever you're saying "thank you" for, be specific about it. This tells your high performers, "I'm paying attention to you. You're really important here and I want to acknowledge that by saying thank you." The bonus is that by being specific, you're also making it a useful thank you. By thanking these good employees for very specific events, they're going to walk out of your office feeling great, but they will also be thinking, "OK. So those extra data analyses that I put in the report (or getting the report done ahead of schedule, etc.) were a really great thing to do. I'm going to make sure I do even more of that."

Of course, saying "thank you" is an inherently nice activity to perform with your high and middle performers. But there are a few other reasons why this is such an important activity to undertake *before* you start tackling the difficult personalities.

#1: Saying "thank you" to high and middle performers stops low performers from spreading negativity.

If you conduct these 'thank you' conversations correctly, your high and middle performers will leave your office feeling motivated and energized. (It feels really good to have the boss call you into a meeting just to say, "thank you.") This positive energy will inoculate high and middle performers against any negativity that might emanate from low performers when it's their turn to talk to you. It's kind of like an 'emotional flu shot' that protects good employees from any negativity viruses that may spread from your difficult personalities.

Difficult personalities love to spread their drama, negativity, denial, blame, excuses and more onto others. And when you start managing them, they may try even harder to manipulate everyone around them into thinking negatively about the organization and its leaders—especially you. But meeting with your high and middle performers first, just to say a big "thank you," takes that power away from difficult personalities. They can try to spread their emotional toxicity, but it won't touch your high and middle performers who will still be riding the emotional high of their conversations with you. They aren't going to care what the difficult personalities have to say.

#2: Saying "thank you" to high and middle performers emo tionally isolates difficult personalities.

Spending extra time with your high and middle performers sends a clear message of "this organization values high performers." This means your best people (i.e. not difficult personalities) get the social cache, and emotional boost, that comes from being an acknowledged high performer.

Meanwhile, your difficult personalities are receiving a very different message; that something they're doing (e.g. their drama, negativity, blaming, etc.) is lowering their status in the minds of their leaders. Most difficult personalities have been coddled for years (many people find it easier to indulge their bad behavior rather than try to do something to stop it). But spending noticeably more time with your high and middle performers sends a clear message that the days of coddling are over.

#3: Saying "thank you" to high and middle performers builds momentum that makes tough conversations more effective.

Talking to difficult personalities is never fun, but it's easier to do when you've built up some momentum that sets the tone for these difficult meetings. Thanking your high and middle performers is fun, and it builds up your mojo and momentum. So by the time you get to your difficult personalities, you'll be mentally insulated, almost like you've had a vaccine against the challenges these low performers are likely to present.

CHAPTER 2

DRAMATICS

The first difficult personality we're going to tackle is the Dramatic Personality, also called a "Dramatic." In part, we start here because Dramatics are fairly straightforward to manage.

We'll be using the FIRE Model from Chapter 1, and we'll learn a new technique called redirection, which will help with several of the difficult personalities. So even if Dramatics aren't a current concern in your workplace, you will want to review this chapter in preparation for later chapters.

Dramatics are those people who crave being the center of attention. Whether it's through a display of exaggerated emotions, telling crisis-driven stories, or some other form of histrionics, they're after recognition and attention. They don't need a major event or happening to try and grab the spotlight. These difficult employees use intense emotions to blow simple events out of proportion. And they're capable of turning even the most benign conversation into a confrontation or competition.

They want a captive audience and for other people to buy into, or better yet, join them in their bad behaviors, which can include gossip, backstabbing, criticism, overreacting, sarcasm and more. Dramatics find all kinds of ways to make their voices heard including making incendiary posts on the organization's internal messaging system, gossiping in the breakroom or creating a scene in meetings. Getting other people hooked on their drama is how they stay the center of attention.

Any leader who has dealt with a Dramatic Personality knows that these low performers are highly skilled at making everyone around them feel frantic and emotionally out of control. And if they succeed in getting you worked-up, frazzled and emotional, it can damage your reputation as a leader.

How Dramatics Process the FIRE Model

Remembering the **FIRE Model** from Chapter 1, we know that we humans generally make sense of the world by observing **Facts**, making **Interpretations** about those facts, then experiencing emotional **Reactions**, which in turn lead to desired **Ends**.

Dramatics also see the world through the lenses of the FIRE Model, but because they like to live in a world filled with histrionics, conflict and drama, this influences their interpretations, reactions and desired ends.

A Dramatic, for example, upon observing the fact that Bob spoke up four times in this morning's meeting, might leap to the interpretation that "Bob is speaking out in meetings in order to make me look bad." The facts by themselves are non-dramatic, but interpretations are wide open to drama.

Next, the Dramatic leaps to an emotional reaction, which might be "Bob is a jerk and a threat, and I am super mad at him." And this leads to a desired end, what the Dramatic desires to happen because of their emotional reaction to the facts. In this case, it might be "I'll start by complaining loudly at this afternoon's team meeting about the unfair allocation of time at meetings. Then I'll spread the rumor that Bob's out to get us all fired."

This is just one example of what the FIRE Model might look like in the brain of the Dramatic. But it's all we need to begin to understand how Dramatic Personalities work and why they are so detrimental to the workplace. The FIRE Model also explains how Dramatics influence other people to attend to, and even join in on, their drama. When attention getting is the goal, saying "Bob is out to undermine us all with how he's taking over meetings. He's plotting to steal everyone's job and we're all going to be out of work by the end of the month," is far more effective than is stating the non-dramatic fact that "Bob spoke up four times in this morning's meeting."

When histrionics and drama infect a workplace, it's typically because our Dramatic Personalities are spiraling the team out of facts and into emotional reactions. While Dramatics enjoy sinister interpretations and catastrophic ends, what they truly love are emotional reactions (and the more emotional, the better). In this way, Dramatic Personalities operate much like social media. The major social media platforms (e.g. Facebook, Twitter and YouTube) want to keep us emotionally 'amped up' because those emotional reactions generate views and clicks, and maybe even 'viral' content.

Wharton professors analyzed nearly 7,000 *New York Times* articles to see what makes an article 'go viral' (in this case making the *New York Times'* most e-mailed list). They found that content that evokes high emotional arousal (e.g. awe, anger or anxiety) is more viral and that content that evokes low-arousal, or deactivating, emotions (e.g., sadness) is less viral. They also found that a one-standard deviation increase in the amount of anger an article evokes increases the odds that it will make the most e-mailed list by 34%.[vii]

You may recall when Facebook expanded its Like button by rolling out six emoji-alternatives called "Reactions" that gave Facebook users a palette of emotions with which to react to posts. The Reactions are "Like," "Love," "Haha," "Yay," "Wow," "Sad" and "Angry." Notice how there's no emoji of a microscope to indicate the reaction that a post is factually accurate? Just as there's no reaction button that asks, "Can we discuss this further?" or that says, "Hey, calm down and think factually before you do or say something you'll regret."

Social media, in all its myriad forms, is training us to react emotionally. Much like the Dramatic Personalities in our office, social media platforms are designed to influence users to feel emotions including awe, anger, anxiety and more. In fact, in the year following their launch, Facebook users shared 300 billion of those Reactions! I'm not sharing this information to try and influence you to eschew all social media. But I do recommend staying aware of the influencers that try to manipulate your emotional reactions, and this includes both Dramatics and social media.

Dramatics love emotional reactions, especially intense and scary emotional reactions, and they want everyone else to live in that world of highly charged emotional reactions with them. That's why it's so important to remain factual (and thus calm, cool and collected) when managing Dramatics. We need to remind ourselves to think factually because that's where we're smarter, more in control, and less likely to say something harmful.

If you want a workplace that's filled with calm professionalism, it's best to live in the world of facts. Because even when facts are objectively bad, they're still easier to handle than a bunch of catastrophizing interpretations, reactions and ends.

Redirection

The second tool we need for managing Dramatics is redirection. All that really means is that when a Dramatic Personality tries to get us to focus on emotional reactions, we're simply going to redirect and refocus the conversation back to facts. And the way we're going to use redirection is by repeating some version the phrase "Just the facts, please."

Redirecting Dramatics to the facts forces them to remain a strict observer of objective reality; only that which can be videotaped, transcribed or otherwise documented and measured. Keeping Dramatics focused on the facts prevents them from making the dangerous leap into the interpretations, reactions and desired ends that fuel their drama. When conversations stay strictly facts-focused, you can address the Dramatic and their bad behaviors without getting caught up in the drama yourself.

For example, imagine a Dramatic Personality storms into our office and histrionically exclaims "I can't keep working like this! No one has ever treated me this disrespectfully in my entire life! I feel like I'm dying inside!" This sounds bad, but we actually have no idea what's really going on. We need to elicit some facts before we can accurately assess the situation. So we're going to redirect this conversation by saying "I have no idea what's going on, so please back up and just give me the facts, please." Or, if we want to take a more empathic approach, we could say, "I hear that you feel upset, but I need to know the facts about what happened, please."

Now, imagine that the Dramatic employee somewhat ignores the request for facts and says "I just spoke with our biggest client and they were so rude and insulting! They're just the worst people to deal with. I don't know how you let them speak to us like this!" We've got a tiny bit more information (i.e. they spoke with our biggest client), but we're still very much in the dark about what the client specifically said, who spoke first, who called whom, what the issue was, etc.

When this happens, we need to redirect the conversation again by saying "Just the facts, please. Start at the beginning and walk me through who initiated the call, what prompted the call, what exactly was said, etc."

The goal in redirecting this conversation is twofold. First, we want to keep ourselves and the Dramatic employee focused entirely on facts, not emotional reactions. If we start feeling angry or agitated by this supposedly disrespectful client, the Dramatic Personality has achieved their goal (i.e. inflaming our emotions and exacerbating the situation).

Second, by redirecting the conversation, we're gently teaching the Dramatic employee that we're not going to listen to their drama. We're letting them know that if they want to storm into our office with a problem, they better know the facts surrounding that issue.

Redirection is typically not a "one-time and done" tool. The first few times you deal with a Dramatic employee, you may need to literally say "Just the facts, please" three, four or even five times during the conversation. Over time, these difficult employees will start to get the message that you want the facts without the drama, but again, it may take a couple of interactions to get there.

If you've hit a wall in your conversation and you've said "Just the facts, please" five times with no success, then it's time to end the conversation. Do this by saying "I need to hear some facts before I can be of any assistance. Take ten minutes to collect yourself, think through the facts, and then come back and tell me the facts."

For many leaders, this approach can seem a little cold. But think back to Chapter 1 and Mindset Shift #5: You Will Probably Need to Tone Down Your Empathy. Remember the research I shared that showed how, in certain situations, too much empathy can be a bad thing? In the case of managing Dramatics, we need to be calm, cool, a bit aloof, and less empathic. Because if we allow ourselves to start feeling what the Dramatic Personality is feeling, we're going to become dramatic ourselves, and that's precisely what we want to avoid.

Managing Dramatics

When we put these two tools together (the FIRE Model and redirection), we've got a simple, facts-based script that encourages Dramatics toward self-sufficiency while avoiding giving them the attention they want.

Depending on the situation, you may not need to deliver all the steps in the following Dramatics Script, but the one step you must *always* follow is the phrase found in Step #1: "Just the facts, please."

Dramatics Script

Step 1. When you hear a Dramatic Personality start to emotionally ramp up, interrupt them by saying, *"I hear that you feel _______, but I need to know the facts about what happened, please."*
When we start by saying "I hear that you feel ____," we're beginning with a dose of understanding and reflection. Adding this touch of niceness doesn't detract from our goals, and in some cases, it helps to deescalate the spiraling drama. Once we've acknowledged that they're experiencing some intense emotional reactions, we then redirect the conversation by saying "but I need to know the facts about what happened, please."

Step 2. Next, say *"I'm not sure that makes sense to me, but I'm listening."*
Sometimes it's necessary to use redirection a few times to get the desired results. And while we're going through that process, it's quite possible that the Dramatic Personality will continue to make some outlandish statements. (We saw this in the example above when the Dramatic said "I just spoke with our biggest client and they were so rude and insulting! They're just the worst people to deal with. I don't know how you let them speak to us like this!")

When we say, "I'm not sure that makes sense to me," we're subtly telling the Dramatic Personality that they're going a bit off-the-rails while also reinforcing that they need to get back to the world of facts.

Step 3. Next, say *"I have 5 minutes to listen, and then I need to move on."*
In addition to redirecting Dramatics multiple times, you may also need to set a limit for how long you're willing to listen to anything that isn't a fact. If they're speaking factually and

you need this information, then obviously, let them talk. But if you're having trouble getting them out of their drama spiral, and they're fighting your attempts at redirection, then you need to get a little firmer. Setting a time limit is an easy way to do that.

Step 4. Once a facts-based discussion is established, say *"How could you take care of this problem by yourself? I trust that you can handle it alone."*

After redirecting the conversation to a discussion of only the facts, it's time to further lead this person towards self-sufficiency. If you intercede when Dramatics bring you drama, you're positively reinforcing them for their undesirable behavior, so be very careful about when you do, and do not, intercede. Whenever a Dramatic brings you an issue, ask yourself "If I intervene right now, am I teaching this person to be more dependent on me or am I teaching them to become more self-sufficient, and thus ultimately less dramatic?"

If the goal is to help this person become less dramatic, we need to challenge them to solve issues on their own. Of course, we need to use good managerial judgement here; if the building is on fire, don't tell them to handle it on their own. But in the case of our customer who was 'so rude and insulting,' this should be a situation where our Dramatic employee can take some independent action. Because if you positively know that you can't trust them to handle this situation, then I must ask, why is this person still on your team?

The Dramatics Script is most effective when used in a one-on-one scenario. Remember, audiences empower Dramatics, so take a deep breath (instead of letting the Dramatic trigger you into emotionally unloading on the spot) and invite these employees into a private meeting before you begin.

The Dramatics Script in Action

Admittedly, the following scenario is a little ridiculous. But when you learn to work through the more bizarre cases of dramatic behavior, the more "normal" situations become significantly easier.

Imagine a scenario where Pat, a Dramatic Personality, comes into the boss's office and, along with lots of exaggerated posturing and crazy hand motions, says:

> *"Oh my gosh! Something horrible just happened! There's water all over my desk and I think the roof is going to collapse! This whole building is unsafe and we're all probably going to die in here! I told you headquarters has never cared about us as employees! We should sound an alarm, and everyone should evacuate the building. You have no idea how bad it is. The building will probably have to be condemned!"*

A good look around the office shows a dry and calmly functioning workplace. This informs the boss that Pat is bringing way more drama than facts. And when the FIRE Model is applied to what Pat just said, it's easy to identify the **F**acts, **I**nterpretations, **R**eactions and desired **E**nds.

The only fact that Pat just shared is that there's water on the desk. Pat's interpretations of that fact are that the roof is going to collapse, that everyone will perish, and that headquarters doesn't care about the employees. Pat's emotional reactions to these interpretations are to feel frantic and anxious; emotions that Pat is eager for the boss to also feel. And Pat's desired end is to evacuate and condemn the building.

Pat has clearly left the world of facts and jumped into the IRE (Interpretations, Reactions and Ends). Given all this, what's the boss's next move?

Let's look at two examples (bad and good) of the boss interacting with Pat in this situation. The first (bad) example shows the boss wrongly trying to directly confront Pat about the drama. As we'll see, confrontation only worsens the situation.

In the second (good) example, the boss uses the Dramatics Script, including the phrase, "Just the facts, please." Using the FIRE Model and redirection diffuses the chaos and disruption that Dramatics bring.

Example #1 (Bad): The boss uses direct confrontation which creates more drama.

Boss: "You need to calm down, Pat. Please go deal with the situation and get back to work."

Pat: "But people might be in danger. You need to do something."

Boss: "I can see from here that things are not as bad as you say. You're not even wet. I don't have time for this right now. Please, just stop with the dramatics."

Pat: "I'm really quite offended that you would say that to me. I believe company policy defines some of what you just said to me as harassment. I'd like to get someone from HR in here because what I hear you saying is that I'm a liar and that you don't care about my personal welfare."

Boss: "That's not what I said. Please, whatever happened out there, just call custodial and have it cleaned up and then get back to work."

Pat: "I really can't believe that you care so little for me, or the rest of the team. And I'm offended that you so blatantly just called me a liar."

Boss: "You're blowing this way out of proportion, Pat. What I'm trying to say, if you'd just listen, is..."

Pat: "Oh, I'm listening. I heard everything you just said, and that's exactly why I'm headed straight to HR."

It didn't take long for this situation to spiral emotionally, which is what the Dramatic wants. If the boss continues in this direction, things will only get worse.

Dramatics don't respond constructively to direct confrontation. They don't see themselves as part of the problem and they will only grow indignant and even more problematic if you try to confront them.

Example #2 (Good): The boss follows the Dramatics Script and uses redirection to shut down the Dramatic.

Boss: "I hear that you are upset, Pat, but I need to know just the facts, please. Can you tell me exactly what happened?"

Pat: "It was just awful. I was so scared."

Boss: "I hear that you're scared and upset, but I really need to hear just the facts, please."

Pat: "There was a lot of water; something needs to be done."

Boss: "OK. I've only got five minutes and then I've got to move onto something else. So please, tell me just the facts."

Pat: "I have no idea where the water came from, but it was on my desk."

Boss: "Again, I'm only interested in hearing the facts. Tell me, exactly how much water is on your desk right now? Is the entire desk covered or is it a small puddle, like a glass of water got knocked over?"

Pat: "Well, I guess it's like a glass of water got knocked over, but I have no idea where it came from. There might be a leak in the roof, or maybe someone poured water on my desk. Why would someone do that to me?"

Boss: "OK, so the only fact you just shared with me is that there's about a glassful of water on your desk. Is that correct?"

Pat: "Yes. At least last time I looked."

Boss: "OK. So first, I want you to go get a towel and wipe up the water. Then, take a few minutes to assess the situation further. If there is a leak in the roof, you can come and let me know that. But I only want you to report back to me with facts. Can we agree to that?"

Pat: "Yeah, I guess..."

Boss: "I believe that once you get the facts you will be able to find a solution to this on your own. If you need help cleaning up the water, you know the extension for custodial, correct?"

Pat: "I guess I'll just have to deal with the situation myself." (Pat leaves the boss's office.)

The Dramatics Script, which focuses around the phrase "Just the facts, please," works because Dramatics can't spiral into ever more intense emotions when we stay calm and facts focused. They want us to get all amped up and dramatic like they are.

By calmly repeating "Just the facts, please," the boss sends Pat a clear and non-confrontational message that the only thing open to discussion is the facts. Drama, conjecture, crazy emotions, histrionics and catastrophizing are not up for discussion. And as we see in the resolution of Example #2, that's usually enough to deflate a Dramatic Personality.

The bonus of using the Dramatics Script is that by staying focused on just the facts, you make yourself a less appealing target for the Dramatic. When attention getting is the goal, it's no fun to be around someone who refuses to give you the spotlight. Consequently, Dramatics are going to think twice before bringing drama to you again.

If you let the Dramatic suck you into interpretations and reactions and desired ends, as we saw in Example 1, they will take you on a non-productive and frustrating emotional ride. But if you use redirection to stay facts focused, Dramatic Personalities will quickly get the message that they can't manipulate you.

There's one more benefit to this approach; we're actually helping the Dramatic gain more emotional control. In effect, this approach is teaching the Dramatic Personality how to respond when they feel their emotional reactions gain steam and start taking over. It may take multiple rounds of "Just the facts, please," spread over time, before you see a more lasting change in their behavior. But with enough discipline, it will likely come eventually.

A Final Wrinkle

What happens if the problem appears solved, but then the Dramatic leaves your office and starts riling-up the other employees? Or if they start bad-mouthing you for being an insensitive jerk?

First, if you followed the approach in Chapter 1 whereby you've had 'thank you' conversations with all your high and middle performers, the risk of drama infecting the rest of your team is significantly lower. Sure, the Dramatic Personality may try to rile-up the rest of the team, but their efforts are unlikely to be all that successful.

Second, in general, Dramatic employees will respond quickly to the approach outlined here because while they love drama, they're not the most aggressive difficult personality. When you've made it clear that drama isn't acceptable, that's usually enough to stop them from escalating things further.

Occasionally, you may come across a Dramatic who wants to keep pushing an issue; the more you try to squash the drama, the more oppositional they become. In those cases, you're no longer dealing with a Dramatic. Rather, you're facing a full-fledged Talented Terror. When this happens, it's time to turn to Chapter 10 which offers a significantly more assertive approach to managing this type of difficult personality.

CHAPTER 3

NEGATIVE PERSONALITIES

We've all been in those meetings where most people are trying to do something positive and constructive, but there's that one difficult personality who keeps sniping and oozing negativity over every good idea. Maybe someone says, "I think this new software will really help our productivity," but the Negative Personality snaps back and says, "Oh please, this company never gets new technology right," thus casting a pall over the rest of the meeting. And that pall, in turn, can stifle creativity, innovation, growth into new markets, confidence, optimism, enthusiasm, and everything else that it takes to win in business.

The Negative Personality is the person who expects the worst. Their negative worldview could be due to any number of personal issues, but since we're not here to play therapist, it's not our concern how they got that way. Our only focus is on keeping the workplace free from their negative behaviors.

The FIRE Model, explained in detail in Chapter 1, shows us that when we see a set of facts, some objective reality, our brain, drawing from our personal past experiences and knowledge, almost immediately makes an interpretation about that fact. This interpretation causes us to have an emotional reaction which then leads to some desired end state that we wish would occur.

So, as an example of the FIRE Model in action, if our company is introducing a new software platform, that is a fact. Once presented with this fact, we might make the interpretation that this new software is good thing. Our emotional reaction to that interpretation might be "I'm excited to learn about the new software," followed by a desired end of "I'd like to help roll out the new software platform to make the transition smoother for everyone."

That's one way the FIRE Model might work. But Negative Personalities experience something quite different when they make the leap from facts to interpretations to reactions to desired ends. Because they view the world through a negatively skewed lens, they filter the facts through a set of irrational beliefs or cognitive distortions. This leads to negative interpretations of the facts resulting in negative emotional reactions and negative desired ends.

The Negative Personality, for example, may leap from the fact that the company is introducing a new software platform to the negative interpretation that the new software is going to fail. This, in turn, may lead to a negative emotional reaction of "I'm dreading this change because it's going to make my work so much harder." And the negative desired end might be, "I'm going to publicly protest the new software by telling everyone that we're doomed to failure if we use it."

The Negative Personality moves from facts to interpretations to reactions to desired ends so quickly that it often catches their managers off guard. And if that negativity spreads through the workplace, it will trigger a host of issues including distrust and decreased engagement and productivity. Managers must be proactive in shutting down the Negative Personality and encouraging a culture of positivity.

Directly attacking the negativity won't work. Trying to manage a Negative Personality by saying, "You're being irrational," or

"Stop being so darn negative," will only increase the negativity. You're not going to change anything with an argument. Instead, we need to address the underlying negative assumptions that drive their negativity. We're not trying to "fix" the person, we're just guiding the Negative Personality in debunking their irrational assumptions and cognitive distortions about the facts so they can make a normal, positive leap from facts to interpretations.

Sadly, negativity bombs are being launched more frequently these days. One of my recent studies, called *Fake News Hits The Workplace,* surveyed more than 3,000 leaders about lying and other bad behaviors in the workplace.[viii] Among the many findings, we discovered that 53% of people have seen an increase in Criticism, 48% have seen an increase in Dismissing others' ideas and 36% have seen an increase in Hostility or disparaging others. So if you've been feeling like there's more vitriol and negativity these days, the data shows that you're right, and it's impacting our workplaces.

Managing Negative Personalities

Managing Negative Personalities begins by debunking their irrational assumptions about the facts. Those irrational assumptions are what fuel their wild leap from objective, unemotional facts to emotionally negative interpretations. Unless the negative assumptions are eradicated, the Negative Personality will never be open to considering new and more positive possibilities.

All this might sound a bit complicated because you've probably already tried to convince Negative Personalities that they were wrong and failed. But this time you won't be trying to convince or force them to change their minds. Instead, you'll be using a five-step process that's built around the question "I'm curious, what facts brought you to that conclusion?" These nine words present a subtle way of challenging Negative Personalities to defend, or otherwise abandon, their irrational assumptions and cognitive distortions.

When you ask a Negative Personality to consider whether they have any factual support for their negativity, they will typically realize that they don't. And even when they can name some facts (e.g. "The last software we implemented went so badly that the company paid to have it uninstalled"), you will typically still have room to push back (e.g. "That's true, but don't we have a different team of leaders now? And is it really true that all technology installs go poorly?").

I'm sometimes asked, "What do I do if a Negative Personality is correct in their negative thinking (e.g. "We always fail at change")?" And my response is that because of the abundance of black-and-white thinking employed by Negative Personalities, it's unlikely that they're correct that your company ALWAYS does anything.

Black-and-white thinking is a cognitive distortion whereby someone views the world in terms of either/or. Something is either good or bad, all or nothing, smart or stupid, a success or a failure. Black-and-white thinking misses that there are typically several shades of gray that exist between black and white. By seeing only two possible options (e.g. right or wrong) this person is missing the middle ground, which is typically where we find reality.

Is it possible, for example, that a company always fails at change? Think about what that would actually mean. A company that always fails at change could never have had even one tiny little success with any type of change; no new iPhones, no new operating systems, no new computers. That's what "always" means, and it doesn't sound like a company that would still be in business.

Plus, consider the word *fail* as in "this company always fails at change." What does fail really mean? Is lagging five minutes behind schedule a failure? Is being less profitable than we hoped a failure? Is installing 'buggy' software that unintentionally taught our employees debugging a failure?

My point is that most things in life come in shades of gray, not black or white. When we limit ourselves to black-and-white thinking, we become more emotional, dogmatic, rigid and fragile as well as less intellectually flexible and creative. Negative Personalities engage in a lot of black- and-white thinking, and that's why it's rare that their negative utterances can withstand real factual scrutiny.

To give you a quick cheat sheet, here are some words that generally indicate the speaker is engaging in black-and-white thinking: *all, always, entirely, every, everybody, failure, fatal, final, impossible, irrevocable, never, nobody, none, total, ultimate,* and *wrong.* When you hear someone say any of those words, or any words like them, just ask them "I'm curious, what facts brought you to that conclusion?"

The phrase, "I'm curious, what facts brought you to that conclusion?" works in a lot of situations. But there will be times when you need to probe and reframe even further. When this happens, use the following five-step Negative Personalities Script for gently debunking irrational beliefs and cognitive distortions. This script leads Negative Personalities to take ownership for the consequences of their negativity, so they have no choice but to rewrite their negative beliefs.

Negative Personalities Script

Step 1: Establish the supposedly negative event that is happening.
This step is usually quite simple. Just listen for the Negative Personality to say some version of, "This terrible, negative thing is happening, and I think it's horrible."

Step 2: Ask the Negative Personality *"I'm curious, what facts brought you to that conclusion?"*
The initial response to this question will typically involve lots of negative black-and-white language, for example "Change *always* fails," or "Bob is *never* correct," or "This deadline is

impossible," or "*Nobody* ever gets promoted here," and so on. It can be tempting at this point to dive right in and start debunking the negativity. But I recommend first asking some gentle clarifying questions that will surface any extra negative thoughts. For example, "What changes are you thinking of when you say that change always fails here?" Or, "I'm curious what you mean when you say this deadline is impossible?"

Step 3: Ask: *"Given your underlying assumptions about this, what is going to happen to you and how will that make you feel?"*
The reality of holding negative beliefs is a significantly less happy and satisfying existence. Here, we want the Negative Personality to acknowledge that their current negative beliefs are not going to help them to be happier or more successful. Leading the Negative Personality to admit the futility of their negativity is helpful in terms of debunking their negative thoughts.

Step 4: Ask *"Are there facts that are contrary to these beliefs?"*
In Step 4, we're actively seeking out facts to debunk the negativity. If the Negative Personality has said, for example, that "Change always fails here," our goal is to help them to find examples of change that wasn't a total failure. This will often involve some back and forth conversing.

The Negative Personality may say "I can't think of any facts that are contrary to these beliefs (e.g. "I can't think of any changes that didn't fail")." If this happens, offer an example (e.g. "How about the time we increased the number of paid vacation days for employees?") and then turn the conversation back over to them by saying "Can you think of another example like that one?"

Step 5: Have the Negative Personality write new rational replacements for the assumptions, or "evidence" uncovered in Step 2.
The final step amounts to the Negative Personality admitting that their negative assumptions were wrong and generating a rewrite. For example, "I concede that there are facts that disprove my old beliefs that "all change fails." I am now open to the possibility that this time the change could work."

On the surface, all you're doing when using the Negative Personalities Script is asking some simple questions from a position of friendly curiosity. But beneath the surface, these questions reveal the Negative Personality to be devoid of facts and suffering from a host of cognitive distortions. By gently exposing the Negative Personality, you evidence compassion while showing them that there's no rational reason to be negative.

Using the Negative Personalities Script in a Group Setting

It's important to note that Negative Personalities will often act out in group settings such as meetings, the company break room, or on the organization's internal messaging system. Negativity is powerfully persuasive, so it's important, in these types of group situations, to act publicly when debunking the negativity. This is different from managing Dramatic Personalities where a one-on-one approach is preferable.

You're now playing to a group and not just the individual Negative Personality. If you want to prevent the negativity from spreading, you must gently reveal the spurious (or nonexistent) factual evidence for the negative interpretations so everyone can hear.

The simple nine-word phrase, "I'm curious, what facts brought you to that conclusion?" as well as the Negative Personalities Script work just as well in group settings as they do in one-on-one conversations. We're just asking a simple question, from a position of curiosity, but it's also a question that will reveal the negative person to be a factually hollow fount of ill will. Once again, by gently exposing the Negative Personality, you show compassion while making it clear to everyone present that there's no rational reason to be negative.

The Negative Personalities Script in Action

Imagine a scenario where ACME Company has just gone through a restructuring that includes personnel changes. Pat, an ACME employee, has just learned that he is getting a new boss. Pat quickly leaps from that fact to the interpretation "Having a new boss is a really bad thing."

Let's look at two examples (bad and good) of Pat's current boss interacting with Pat in this situation. In the first (bad) example, the boss directly confronts Pat's negativity which only worsens the situation.

In the second (good) example, the boss gently debunks Pat's negativity by using the five-step Negative Personalities Script, which centers around the phrase "I'm curious, what facts brought you to that conclusion?"

Example #1 (Bad): The boss directly confronts Pat's negativity.

Pat: "I just heard that I'm getting a new boss. We really need to talk about this because it basically means that my career here is over."

Boss: "I think you're making the situation out to be a lot worse than it really is, Pat. Why don't you think of this as a great opportunity to work with someone who will challenge you in new ways?

I'll always be here as a sounding board if you need me, but this is what the company has decided."

Pat: "You don't understand. I can't make this kind of change. It's going to destroy everything I've worked for."

Boss: "That's nonsense, Pat. You're in charge of your career and that includes creating your own successes. You need to stop being so negative all the time. You're only going to make this transition harder for yourself and for others with that kind of attitude."

Pat: "I am looking out for the others. We're all going to suffer due to these unnecessary changes. But now I can see that you're against me, too."

In this example, the boss only worsens the situation by directly confronting Pat's anxiety. Saying things like "Stop being so negative" only increases the fear and anxiety that's fueling Pat's irrational assumptions. And telling Pat that "everything will be OK" won't help to change his negative viewpoint. Even if the boss really knows that everything will be OK, it's not OK right now for Pat, and in this moment, that's all that Pat can see, feel and hear.

The only sure way to get Pat to make the leap from fact to positive interpretation is to debunk any negative assumptions.

Example #2 (Good): The boss follows the Negative Personali ties Script and gently debunks Pat's negativity.

Pat: "I just heard that I'm getting a new boss. We really need to talk about this because it basically means that my career here is over."

Boss: "I'm just curious, Pat, what facts bring you to that conclusion?"

Pat: "It's just always how it works out."

Boss: "I'm confused, what's always how what works out?"

Pat: "Change never works out for me. If I get a new boss, my career is over because there's no way the new boss is going to recognize my skills and talents."

Note: Up to this point, the Negative Personalities Script has allowed the boss to surface Pat's negative underlying assumptions (i.e. all change is bad for me, the new boss won't recognize my skills and talents, the Boss is the only one who controls my career and happiness). The next steps will focus on gently debunking and rewriting those negative assumptions.

Boss: "So, and again, I'm just curious here, if you really believe all those things, what is going to happen to you and how will it make you feel?"

Pat: "Like I said, this is going to ruin my career which means my life is going to stink."

Boss: "Is that what you want; for your career to end and for your life to stink?"

Pat: "Of course not. I've worked really hard to get where I am today."

Boss: "That's true, you have worked really hard to get where you are today. So let's take a look at some of the assumptions that you've just shared with me. Let's start with your statement that change never works out for you."

Pat: "It's true."

Boss: "Are you sure about that, because didn't you walk into work yesterday all excited about the new analytics software that just got released?"

Note: One way to debunk irrational underlying assumptions is to look for counter examples of those underlying assumptions. Here, the boss is debunking Pat's underlying assumption that all change is bad by helping Pat to find situations where change wasn't bad.

Pat: "Yeah, but what does that have to do with getting a new boss?"

Boss: "Well, the new analytics software is a change, isn't it?"

Pat: "That's a different kind of change."

Boss: "How about back in the day before cell phones and email when the company used to give us a calling card and we had to use public payphones to make our calls? Do you remember that?"

Pat: "That was awful. Most of the payphones didn't work and there was never any privacy."

Boss: "But now the company gives you an iPhone to use instead. It sounds like you prefer the change of using your iPhone to making calls from payphones."

Pat: "OK, so the iPhone was a good change. But I still don't see how it's comparable to getting a new boss."

Boss: "Right now we're just looking for examples of times when change did work for you. Doesn't your current car drive a lot faster while getting lower mileage than any car you drove 20 years ago?"

Pat: "Yes."

Boss: "And speaking of 20 years ago, don't you have a bigger title in the organization now, along with a bigger salary, than you did back then?"

Pat: "OK. I see what you're getting at. I guess some change is actually good."

Boss: "It sounds like you've experienced a number of changes that worked out well for you."

Pat: "You're right. I just never thought of it that way before."

Boss: "This makes me curious about your belief that you can't adapt to a new boss and that getting a new boss is going to end your career. I seem to recall that you weren't so sure it would work out when we first started working together. Am I right?"

Pat: "Yes, but I really like having you as my boss. That's my whole issue here."

Boss: "I hear that, but you do agree that it's true that you've adapted to a new boss before and it's worked out well for you."

Pat: "Yes, that is true."

Boss: "And how about this notion that getting a new boss will end your career and that your talents won't be recognized? Do you remember when you worked on the Globex project? I didn't give you the green light or anything. You just went ahead and did it on your own, and everyone in organization agreed that you did an amazing job."

Pat: "That's true. I really loved working on that project."

Boss: "And you did a great job. So isn't that an example of you being in total control of your own career and your own happiness?"

Pat: "I understand what you're saying. I have done this before, and I guess I'll do it again. I just wish I didn't have to."

Boss: "Then let's talk about some strategies for making this a positive change. Does that sound OK?"

Pat: "Yeah, that sounds good. And thanks. I really appreciate your help."

A Final Wrinkle

We learned that when the Negative Personality says something like, "Our company always fails at change," their utterance is loaded with irrational assumptions and cognitive distortions. And we've got the script to debunk, reframe and restructure their negativity.

But what if after all our good work handling the negativity, there are still some facts that suggest our company might actually struggle with this new change initiative? What if, after we stripped away the distorted negativity, there were still facts about which we should legitimately be concerned?

This is a good place to engage our Negative Personality in helping us develop a solution (and repurpose the energy that was previously directed solely towards highlighting potential problems). After you've used the Negative Personalities Script, try asking them "How will we make sure that we succeed?" You can use this question one-on-one, but it also works extremely well in a group setting because it engages the positive thinkers and the problem solvers to develop answers that the Negative Personality will often have missed.

CHAPTER 4

BLAMERS

Blamers are difficult personalities who only emerge when something goes wrong. Blamers are not in denial; they do recognize that something has gone wrong. But whether the Blamer is totally at fault for what went wrong, or only partially responsible, these difficult personalities try and deflect the responsibility for the issue onto somebody else.

Blame is different from excuses. Blame targets a person (e.g. "I didn't finish the report because Bob didn't get me the right data") while excuses target a thing (e.g. "I didn't finish the report because the internet was down"). Blamers throw other people under the bus to try and shift the attention away from themselves. It's like a magician distracting the audience while they're pulling off the real trick somewhere else. The Blamer's goal is "Don't look at me, look over there at that person instead."

Blame is an aggressive stance; it's aggressive and attacking and that makes it dangerous to have in the workplace. While excuses are not a good thing, they're often slightly less damaging to the organization's culture than blame. Making an excuse like "the internet crashed," which points fingers at an inanimate object, is typically less harmful than casting aspersions about another person (or group of people). Those 'other people' will learn of the blame, hurt feelings will result, and they may reciprocate the blame, causing the blame to grow.

Research shows us that blame is socially contagious. Formally called the "blame contagion," it's basically where somebody sees blame used to avoid accountability and then thinks, "Look at how that person just used blame to avoid taking accountability for their mistake. What a good idea. I think I'll use blame the next time I mess up!"

A study out of the University of Southern California and Stanford University asked people to read about a special election called by then California Governor, Arnold Schwarzenegger.[ix] Schwarzenegger had called the expensive special election to pass four propositions that were all thoroughly defeated.

One group of research subjects read a version of the story that quoted Schwarzenegger as saying that responsibility for this debacle rested solely with him. Another group of the research subjects read a version of the story in which Schwarzenegger blamed special interest groups for the election's failure. Both research groups, after reading their respective stories, followed instructions to write about a time they personally had made a mistake.

The study results showed that the research group that read about Arnold Schwarzenegger blaming other people were significantly more likely to blame other people for their own mistakes. But the group that read the article where Arnold Schwarzenegger took responsibility, when they wrote about a time when they made a mistake, they generally wrote "I made the mistake. It was on me." Just like the article they had read; they took accountability for the mistake instead of placing blame.

The blame contagion study shows that when we hear other people blame, we are more likely to blame others.

Blame has no upside; it doesn't do anything positive for anyone. Blame is a dangerous emotional reaction. It's aggressive, it's angry, and it's contagious. Learning to manage Blamers isn't just a way to avoid having to deal with these difficult personalities. When incorrectly managed, Blamers can infect the whole workplace.

Managing Blamers

Unlike people who are in denial, which is declaring something to be untrue, Blamers do know that something has gone wrong. But instead of taking accountability for that mistake or error, Blamers try and deflect the responsibility to somebody else. It's because Blamers do know that something happened that we're given an opening though which we can redirect these difficult personalities from blame to problem solving. (You can find a detailed explanation of redirection in Chapter 2.)

Blamers typically excel at derailing conversations and sending them in another direction. Stopping the blame requires limiting conversations to only those things over which these difficult personalities actually have some control. The phrase "Let's discuss what we CAN control" redirects the conversation back to the real problem by clearly expressing the message, "I don't want to talk about anyone else. I only want to talk about what you and I have control over right here, right now."

You may need to repeat this phrase a few times until the Blamer gets the message that there's no escaping this topic. But when used consistently, the phrase "Let's discuss what we CAN control" is typically all it takes to redirect Blamers to a place of accountability.

This phrase is just as effective with occasional Blamers as it is with habitual Blamers. And after a Blamer hears you repeat the phrase "Let's discuss what we CAN control," they will start to recognize you as someone who does not tolerate blame. You're effectively shutting down their favorite escape route from accountability, which means that they're a lot less likely to use blame around you ever again.

The Phrase "Let's discuss what we CAN control" in Action

Imagine a scenario where an employee, Pat, is late in turning in an important report. The boss calls Pat into her office to discuss the late report, but Pat refuses to take any accountability for the situation. Instead, Pat puts all the blame on a coworker named Bob.

Let's look at two examples (bad and good) of the boss interacting with Pat. The first (bad) example shows a common trap where Pat sucks the boss into an unproductive blame conversation.

In the second (good) example, the boss uses the phrase, "Let's discuss what we CAN control" to effectively redirect Pat to a place of accountability.

Example #1 (Bad): Pat sucks the boss into a blame conversation.

Boss: "Pat, the report I needed from you is past deadline."

Pat: "Well, that's not my fault because Bob in Accounting didn't give me the final data to finish the report on time."

Boss: "Did you follow up with Bob when you realized you were missing the data?"

Pat: "You know what it's like trying to work with Bob. Remember the time you were working on the ACME report and he didn't get you the data you needed until the end of the day on a Friday? You had to work all weekend because of Bob. Boy, were you angry!"

Boss: "That was a mess. Look, I know Bob can sometimes be tough to work with, but..."

It didn't take long for Pat to win this conversation. The boss's intention may have been to confront Pat about the missing report but blame quickly derailed the conversation. Pat used blame to sidestep accountability by steering the boss into a conversation about Bob and how tough it is to work with him. And now that the boss has joined forces with Pat in blaming Bob, it's going to be difficult to turn the focus back to Pat's accountability for the missing report.

If the Blamer delivers their blame with enough intensity, and you're not prepared to redirect with the phrase "Let's talk about what we CAN control," the Blamer can easily suck you into an unproductive and potentially dangerous blame conversation.

Example #2 (Good): The boss redirects the conversation with the phrase "Let's discuss what we CAN control."

Boss: "Pat, the report I needed from you is past deadline."

Pat: "Well, that's not my fault because Bob in Accounting didn't give me the final data to finish the report on time."

Boss: "OK, I hear that, but I don't want to talk about Bob. Let's just discuss what we CAN control."

Pat: "I don't control anything in this situation. Bob screwed this one up, not me. You should really go talk to Bob."

Boss: "I don't want to talk to Bob. I want to talk to you, and I want us to discuss what we CAN control."

Pat: "It's not my fault. I don't control Bob. Why do you keep insisting that I have some control here?"

Boss: "Because there are things that you do control."

Pat: "Like what?"

Boss: "Would you agree that you control your own reactions?

Pat: "Of course I control my own reactions. But what am I supposed to do when Bob messes up and makes me look bad?"

Boss: "Let's start with your reaction to Bob, which as you just said is something that you do control."

Pat: "You know Bob is really hard to work with; you've experienced that yourself. Sure, so maybe sometimes I avoid talking to him because I don't want to deal with him. But no one wants to work with Bob. It's not just me."

Boss: "So you agree that you do control your reactions?"

Pat: "Yes, but..."

Boss: "Terrific. That's a great place to start. So what's another, more positive way that you can react when you need something from Bob?"

Pat: "I suppose I could message him, or even email him the next time I need something from him."

When you peel back the layers of blame with the phrase "Let's talk about what we CAN control," there's always something over which the Blamer has control; even if it's as simple as having control over the reaction to a situation.

Control is exactly what the Blamer wants to avoid. They've acknowledged that something has gone wrong, but they want to deflect the responsibility to someone else. They don't want to take ownership. It's your job to guide the Blamer to accountability by saying, "All I want to talk about right now is what we CAN control." And redirection allows you to do just that.

By redirecting the conversation back to the central issue (e.g. what Pat CAN control), the Blamer can no longer dodge accountability. And best of all, redirection allows us to manage the Blamer with some empathy. We're not giving them a vicious reprimand. We're just simply saying, "We're not changing topics, we're not discussing other people, we're only talking about what we CAN control."

CHAPTER 5

PROBLEM BRINGERS

You might have heard the truism that there are two types of people in the world: Problem Bringers and Problem Solvers.

Problem Solvers are those people who, when there's a problem, work hard to find a solution before they ask for help. Problem Bringers, as the name implies, recognize a problem and then immediately bring that problem to someone else to fix, and it's usually a boss or manager. Problem Bringers appear to have no interest in independent problem solving, and that translates to extra work and frustration for anyone leading, or working with, these difficult personalities.

Creating a team of high performing Problem Solvers should be the goal for every manager. Not only will these employees solve more problems, but they'll also be significantly more fulfilled and inspired by their work. And think of all the new business opportunities, productivity improvements, quality advancements and innovations they'll create for you. But before you blame your Problem Bringers for their lack of Problem-Solving ability, it's important to note that sometimes the boss is responsible for encouraging and enabling Problem-Bringer behavior.

Oftentimes, when an organization suffers with Problem Bringers, it's because some level of a Parent/Child style of management exists. The Parent/Child concept comes from a psychological school of thought known as Transactional Analysis. Essentially, this relationship framework is where a manager takes a superior parent or giver role that says: I *give* assignments, I *give* instructions, I *give* feedback (e.g. praise, security, criticism, reward etc.). This treats employees much like children who have no choice other than to *take* feedback and to *take* assignments and to *take* instruction while left passively waiting to be *held* accountable.

Consider, for example, performance appraisals. In the typical company, it's common for the manager to assume a parent role (giving praise, criticism, raises, scores, etc.) while the employee is in child mode, taking and reacting to the feedback. If the employee gets praise, they feel great and have a positive emotional reaction. But if they get criticism, they feel bad and react angrily. When a Parent/Child dynamic exists, regardless of whether the appraisal is good or bad, the employee inhabits a passive and reactive mindset.

The Parent/Child dynamic provides employees with little to no initiative to "be more" and to "do more." It thwarts self-sufficiency, leaving employees feeling powerless over and disengaged about their work life (including the desire to actively problem solve). So if employees lack independence, or if they're deeply dependent on their leaders, it may be a sign that it's time to rethink the style of management that's in use.

It's much better if leaders and employees have an Adult/Adult relationship. And it should be noted that the Parent, Child and Adult roles are not immutable; we can move into different roles with different people, and we can even alter the dynamics of relationships that have existed for years.

When both the manager and the employee are inhabiting Adult roles, it encourages people to become self-sufficient Problem

Solvers. The adult voice is our logical, independent, self-sufficient, rational (calm, cool, collected) voice. This is the person who says, "I will go out into the world and figure out things for myself and I'll do it calmly, coolly, collectively, rationally and self-sufficiently. I will take care of it myself."

Another factor that encourages Problem-Bringer behavior is when managers are more competent at their employees' jobs than are the employees. Most managerial promotions happen because of technical success (and not leadership skills). But being highly skilled can mean thinking (and acting like) you can do things better than your employees. This can be a Problem-Bringer trap. If you find yourself pushing employees aside so you can step in to do their work, or fix their problems and mistakes, you aren't helping them to become Problem Solvers. Instead, you're encouraging Problem-Bringer behavior.

Whenever an employee brings you a problem, you have a decision to make. You can jump in and solve the problem yourself, or you can guide that person in discovering a solution for themselves. I know it can be a big temptation to want to fix things yourself, but this deprives your employees of the opportunity to grow and to learn. And, in turn, it guarantees that your people will keep pestering you for solutions. If you want to turn your Problem Bringers into Problem Solvers, you need to give up some control.

Encouraging Problem-Solver behavior makes a manager's job easier and it helps employees, too. Research shows that individuals who have the greatest sense of control over their own lives, futures, and careers, are the most engaged at work. My research has also found that individuals can drive as much as 94% of their own employee engagement by developing proactivity, resilience, goals, anticipation, curiosity, and optimism. In other words, proactive or optimistic employees can have a great work experience even if they don't have a great boss, because they've learned how to control their own destiny. But when we tell employees that only the boss can make work a good experience, it inadvertently creates a Parent/Child dynamic.

I know this can seem a bit esoteric, so let me put it another way. A generally accepted goal of parenting is to raise kids that can survive and thrive as adults without relying on their parents. If my kids are able-bodied and healthy, and yet they're living on my couch when they're thirty years old, unable to hold down jobs or support themselves, there's a very good chance that I didn't foster in them enough self-sufficiency. Of course, I love my kids, and I want to see them a lot when they're adults, but more than anything, my goal is to ensure that they can survive and thrive as adults without me.

The same basic principle applies to our employees. If we really care about them, we want them sufficiently independent to be great Problem Solvers. We should want our employees to feel a sense of control over their lives and careers. But if they're running to us every time there's a hiccup, they're not evidencing the level of 'adultness' required to fulfill their potential. And frankly, not only is that bad for their careers, it's a nightmarish drain on a leader's time and energy.

Everything I've just said is so intuitive that it would be easy to think that every leader is following this approach. Unfortunately, the data tells us that's not the case. I studied 27,048 executives, managers and employees in a report called "The Risks of Ignoring Employee Feedback."[x] One of the big discoveries was that only 23% of people say that when they share their work problems with their leader, he/she 'Always' responds constructively. By contrast, 17% say their leader 'Never' responds constructively. And overall, more than half of employees feel that their leader doesn't consistently respond constructively when they share their work problems.

Even more shocking is the discovery that if someone says their leader 'Always' responds constructively when they share their work problems, they're about 12 times more likely to recommend the company as a great employer.

Additionally, my study, "How to Build Trust in The Workplace,"[xi] surveyed more than 7,000 people all about why people do, or don't, trust their leaders. And through regression analysis, my team and I discovered that the number one driver of whether an employee will trust their boss is the extent to which they felt that their boss responded constructively when they shared their work problems.

If we want our people to be Problem Solvers, we need to do a great job responding constructively when they bring us problems. This leads to the specific question we're going to ask to turn Problem Bringers into Problem Solvers.

Managing Problem Bringers

The goal in managing Problem Bringers is to lead them towards more independent Problem-Solving behavior. It may sound strenuous, but it actually only requires asking the simple question "What's your plan for solving this issue?"

When an employee comes to you with a problem, you never want to blame them by saying "How could you have let this happen? This is one of our best clients!" Most managers won't openly admit to responding to Problem Bringers in this manner, but we all know that a great many managers regularly hurl similar accusations at their employees. And it doesn't need to be a hurled accusation; often an exasperated sigh or an annoyed wince is all it takes to send a message of blame.

Nor do you want to push Problem Bringers over to the sidelines and insert yourself into the situation as the Problem Solver. Saying "I'll take this over myself; I'm going to call the client directly and I will get this problem straightened out," enfeebles the employee, destroys their confidence, and eliminates any opportunity for accountability and proactivity. You're just keeping that person in Problem-Bringer mode.

The simple question "What's your plan for solving this issue?" establishes an Adult/Adult relationship. With just a few words, you've created a dynamic where two logical, self-sufficient adults, one coaching the other, are focusing on achieving better performance. Asking "What's your plan for solving this issue?" forces Problem Bringers to develop their critical thinking skills, to take initiative and to become proactive. And as these new and positive behaviors become reinforced, and Problem-Solver behavior becomes more habitual, you'll find yourself mired in employee problems less and less.

The Problem Solver Question "What's your plan for solving this issue?" in Action

Imagine a scenario where an employee, Pat, walks into the boss's office and says "Boss, we've got a huge problem with one of our clients and I think we might lose their business."

This is the kind of Problem-Bringer situation that rightly spikes a manager's blood pressure. But as much as the wrong response risks losing the client account, the wrong response also risks ruining the effectiveness, accountability and future growth of the employee.

The first (bad) example shows a Parent/Child interaction where the boss keeps Pat firmly in the role of Problem Bringer.

In the second (good) example, the boss uses the question "What's your plan for solving this issue" to establish an Adult/Adult relationship that encourages Pat towards Problem-Solver behavior.

Example #1 (Bad): The boss keeps Pat in the role of Problem Bringer.

Pat: "Boss, we've got a problem with the ACME account. They're angry about a delivery last week that had damaged product and I think we might lose their business!"

Boss: "Shipping is your department, Pat. I'm really disappointed in you."

Pat: "I'm sorry."

Boss: "Sorry doesn't help right now. ACME is one of our biggest clients and if we lose them, we're going to be in real trouble."

Pat: "I know that. I don't know what to say."

Boss: "Obviously, I'm going to have to put aside everything else and fix this issue with ACME. You and I will talk about this later though, make no mistake. I want to make sure that you understand the gravity of this situation."

Pat: "I do understand. And if I can help in any way..."

Boss: "The best thing you can do right now is to stay out of my way. I'm going to have my hands full fixing this problem."

The boss is understandably upset but scolding Pat and then stepping in to fix the problem is basically treating Pat like a child. The Parent/Child dynamic of this interaction won't allow Pat to gain the confidence or critical thinking skills required for independent problem solving.

Example #2 (Good): The boss uses the question "What's your plan for solving this issue" to encourage Problem-Solver thinking.

Pat: "Boss, we've got a problem with the ACME account. They're angry about a delivery last week that had damaged product and I think we might lose their business!"

Boss: "I know you've worked very hard to get us where we are with that account, so what's your plan for solving this issue, Pat?"

Pat: "I came to you as soon as I got the email from Joan at ACME telling me that most of the product in our last shipment was damaged and that her bosses are freaking out."

Boss: "OK. So, what's your plan for solving the issue?"

Pat: "Joan and I have a pretty strong relationship; that's why she sent me the heads-up email. I'm confident that she can get me a meeting with her bosses on short notice. I'd like to drive over to ACME as soon as we're done here. I believe that a face-to-face meeting that shows our sincere desire to right this wrong is our best shot at smoothing things over."

Boss: "OK. What else does your plan include?"

Pat: "Unfortunately, I think we're going to have to take a loss on this. ACME's clients are depending on them, and they can't deliver because of our error. My idea is we offer to express deliver the product directly to ACME's clients, just this one time. The cost of shipping will set us back a bit, but it allows ACME to save face with their customers, and I believe it will save our relationship with ACME."

Boss: "Is there anything else that you plan to do?"

Pat: "We obviously need to look into why this shipment got damaged. As soon as I settle things with ACME, I'd like to put together an emergency damage control team to investigate why this happened and to fix whatever went wrong, so it doesn't happen again."

Wow! Most employees do have good or even great ideas. But if they don't feel safe sharing those ideas, or if they are shut down by a boss who steps in and takes control whenever a problem occurs, those ideas will never get heard, let alone implemented.

You may know exactly what to do when an employee comes to you with a problem. But by asking "What's your plan for solving this issue" instead of playing the role of fixer, it moves the employee from Problem Bringer to potential Problem Solver. You may have noticed that in the bad example, everything the boss says is a statement. By contrast, in the good example, everything the boss says is a question that encourages Pat to embrace a Problem-Solver mindset.

Initially, this questioning approach may take a little longer than just stepping in and fixing things yourself or telling the employee exactly what to do. It takes some time to sit and listen to someone's ideas for solving a problem. And it's not always easy to keep an open mind when hearing solutions that aren't exactly what you would do in the situation. But taking the extra time to encourage Problem-Solver behavior now means employees will come to you less often with their problems in the future.

CHAPTER 6

OVERLY SENSITIVE PERSONALITIES

If you manage people for long enough, you'll eventually meet the Overly Sensitive Personality. This is the employee who needs some feedback or help, but who is so overly sensitive that they break down if you even look at them the wrong way, let alone give them some tough news.

Overly Sensitive Personalities typically behave this way due to low self-confidence coupled with a strong external locus of control. Locus of control is the degree to which people believe they have control over the outcome of events in their lives. Individuals with a strong internal locus of control believe events in their lives derive primarily from their own actions. But people who have a strong external locus of control, such as Overly Sensitive Personalities, cede that control to external factors, such as a boss or the organization.

Because Overly Sensitive Personalities don't feel personally in control of their lives, it makes them hypervigilant to disapproval and criticism. Without any control, they feel helpless to fix the situation. The good news is that while these difficult personalities can be needy and irritating (especially for hard-charging and tough-minded leaders), they rarely become dangerous.

Managing Overly Sensitive Personalities

The Overly Sensitive Personality isn't the most difficult personality you're ever going to deal with, but you do need to approach these people with a bit of extra care. If you walk into their office, for example, and say, "Your work is not where it needs to be!" they will emotionally break down and you'll never succeed in getting better performance out of them.

Managing Overly Sensitive Personalities requires a gentle touch. You're still going to give them the feedback they need, but it requires a smooth delivery plus a bit of psychological savvy. For this, you're going to use the following Overly Sensitive Personality Script to show these people that they have real potential. Then, you're going to use that potential to set a new standard.

Here's the Overly Sensitive Personalities Script that allows you to do this:

Overly Sensitive Personality Script

Step 1: Start by saying *"I know you have much more potential than you're using. You might not even see this potential in yourself, but I see it."*
Because Overly Sensitive Personalities have low self-confidence, and are hypervigilant to disapproval and criticism, we want to ease our way into this conversation. By using the two statements in Step 1, we're giving them a compliment by highlighting their potential and we're setting the stage to show them how they're not realizing their full potential.

Step 2: Next say *"I know full well you could be doing ____ because I see you've got the talent to achieve it."*
In Step 2, we name the specific thing that we want them to improve upon, but we're placing it in the context of being

something that we're totally confident that they can achieve. For the Overly Sensitive Personality, we want to leave no doubt that they can absolutely achieve the improvements we require.

Step 3: Next say *"Right now, you're not giving enough attention to _____, and as a result your talent isn't being used fully and your performance isn't where it needs to be."*
The word "attention" is the most critical part of this script, because paying attention is a choice. When the Overly Sensitive Personality hears a boss say, "I need you to change X and you need to put more attention on X, Y, Z," that is something that is eminently controllable.

Now, instead of feeling bad about this situation, the employee is thinking, "OK, so I'm not currently meeting my potential, and that news makes me feel kind of bad. But the reason I'm not meeting my potential is that I'm not putting enough attention on something I have total control over which is this issue the boss just mentioned. And if all I have to do is put my attention on X, Y, Z, I'm going to match my performance up to my potential."

This approach is sometimes known as encouraging "mastery thinking," in which we focus on learning, improvement and controllable actions, rather than on outcomes and innate intelligence.

If we tell the Overly Sensitive Personality that the reason their performance is subpar is that they're just not smart enough, we're fomenting a sense of helplessness (i.e. If I'm not innately smart, how can I ever become smarter?). This is the equivalent of telling a basketball player that the reason they're not starting is that they're not tall enough. There's nothing they can realistically do about it.

By contrast, when we tell the Overly Sensitive Personality that the problem is that they're not giving enough attention to a specific issue, that's not something that requires innate talent; it's a simple choice to focus more on this one issue. This gives the Overly Sensitive Personality a strong feeling of optimism that this is an issue on which they can absolutely improve.

The Overly Sensitive Personality Script in Action

Imagine a scenario where the boss has some tough feedback for Pat who is an Overly Sensitive Personality.

In the first (bad) example, the boss delivers the feedback too strongly and Pat cracks.

In the second (good) example, the boss uses the Overly Sensitive Personality Script to positively reinforce Pat's potential and innate talent. The boss then challenges Pat to meet those qualities by giving critical feedback on correctable behaviors.

Example #1 (Bad): The boss's critical feedback is too strong.

Boss: "The reason I called you in here today, Pat, is that you're currently not meeting performance expectations. You'll need to do a better job or there will be consequences."

Pat: "I'm really trying, but obviously I'm just not good enough." (Pat thinks to herself: It feels like the boss is out to get me because of my incompetence, but there's nothing I can do about it because I'm already trying my best.)

Pat's strong external locus of control causes her to interpret the boss's feedback as, "You could be doing more, but you're not doing it because you're not smart enough." Even though intelligence is somewhat malleable, Pat does not believe this. Instead, Pat considers smartness, or intelligence, as an innate trait. And, as an Overly Sensitive Personality, Pat doesn't feel any control over innate traits.

Pat is basically hearing the boss say, "I need you to fix something that you don't have any natural talent to fix." Even if the boss were to say, "You have potential, Pat, but you're not doing a good job and you need to do a better job," it's still not a particularly instructive or helpful approach to take with an Overly Sensitive Personality. The boss may as well be telling Pat to grow another foot taller.

Example #2 (Good): The boss gently uses the Overly Sensitive Personalities Script to deliver critical feedback.

Boss: "Listen, Pat. I know you have much more potential than you're using. You might not even see this potential in yourself, but I see it."

Note: This is the boss addressing Pat's lack of confidence.

Pat: (Thinks to herself: I feel good about what the boss is saying.)

Boss: "I know full well you could be doing a better job calculating the monthly reports because I see you've got the talent to achieve it. Right now, you're not giving enough attention to the numbers on the reports, and as a result your talent isn't being used fully and your performance isn't where it needs to be."

Pat: (Pat nods affirmatively and thinks to herself: I know exactly where I need to pay attention to elevate my game, and I have the potential to do it. This IS something over which I have total control,)

Even though Pat is insecure, and overly sensitive with a strong external locus of control that requires other people's approval, she can still elevate her game because she has total control over it.

Overly Sensitive Personalities are emotionally susceptible to feedback. But when you frame that feedback in a way that gives them the belief that they can succeed, it allows them to hear, process and act on that feedback.

CHAPTER 7

ADVANTAGE-TAKERS

Most of us want to get along with our employees and coworkers and to be helpful, collegial, and friendly. And we certainly don't want the reputation of being the jerk who's never willing to help or who always says "No."

But there are people who will try to take advantage of our good nature and ask us to carry their workload, bend the rules, reveal confidential information, and more. These difficult personalities are Advantage-Takers, and they're particularly common in organizations that embrace a competitive work environment.

Advantage-Takers are always on the lookout for ways to exploit circumstances to gain an advantage, and that includes moving into positions of leadership. If knocking someone else down means they get ahead, that's OK by them. So when you're someone who struggles to say "No," it's like waving an inviting red flag at an Advantage-Taker.

The tricky thing about managing Advantage-Takers is that they're clever manipulators. If you take the wrong approach, they'll wear you down by trying to twist your words and make you look like the bad person. Or they might try and redirect the situation to make it look like you're the Advantage-Taker instead of them.

Managing Advantage-Takers

When an Advantage-Taker tries to exploit your openness and caring, the fastest and most effective way to shut them down is by saying "No." But for most of us, "No" isn't an easy thing to say.

The following Advantage-Taker Script introduces a four-step process to saying "No" that makes it a whole lot easier. Basically, you're going to use the phrase "I hear this is important to you" to acknowledge that the other person's request has been heard while setting a clear path to the firm, but kind "No" that follows.

Advantage-Taker Script

Step 1: Use empathy to protect your reputation.
Alleviate any concerns you have about gaining a 'standoffish' reputation by acknowledging the importance the other person attributes to their request. This simple show of empathy is as easy as saying ***"I hear this is important to you"*** or ***"It's apparent this means a lot to you."***

Step 2: Use the word 'No'.
It may seem obvious but saying the actual word 'No' really is necessary in these situations. Don't equivocate by saying something that softens the 'No' such as "Well, I just don't think so." That just keeps the door open for the Advantage-Taker to move in. And you don't want to give a long-winded reason for your decision to decline. That's just ammunition for the Advantage-Taker to convince you to say 'Yes.' Limit the rationale behind your 'No' to a single, short sentence.

Step 3: Don't apologize for saying 'No.'
Advantage-Takers often prey upon those that they intuit are weaker (or more sensitive, passive or nervous). If you offer

an apology when you say 'No,' the Advantage-Taker may take this as a signal of defeat or weakness. This can encourage an Advantage-Taker to push even harder. Not to mention, you haven't done anything wrong, so there's zero reason to apologize. Saying 'No' to someone who's taking advantage of you, or asking you to break the rules, is not a transgression. It's the right thing to do.

Step 4: Own your decision.
Using the words ***"I won't,"*** or ***"I've decided not to,"*** rather than "I can't," or "I shouldn't," emphasizes that you've made a clear and final decision. Owning your decision is a sign of strength (plus it inoculates against potential future attempts to take advantage of you).

Let's look at some real-life examples of saying "No" to an Advantage-Taker.

The Advantage-Taker Script in Action

Imagine a scenario where a company has just given out bonuses. Each manager in the company received the bonus numbers for their specific employees along with explicit instructions to not share the numbers with anyone else. But then Pat, one of the company's managers, catches Frank, another manager, in the break-room and says "I think my team got shortchanged on the annual bonus. What did your people get?"

Let's look at two examples (bad and good) of Frank interacting with Pat in this situation. In the first (bad) example, Frank wants to say "No," but Pat manipulates him into revealing the confidential information.

In the second (good) example, Frank uses the Advantage-Taker Script to say "No" (in a firm-but-nice manner) when Pat tries to take advantage of him.

Example #1 (Bad): Frank fails to say "No."

Pat: "I think my team got shortchanged on the annual bonus. What did your people get?"

Frank: "I'm not comfortable sharing that information with you. You know we were asked not to."

Pat: "That doesn't mean anything. They just say that to us because HR makes them. Everyone is talking about the bonuses. I just heard Carol say that her people got seven percent! I think that's outrageous, don't you? We both know that our teams work twice as hard as Carol's. So, what did your employees get?"

Frank: "I'm sorry, but I really don't want to say. Actually, this conversation is making me a bit uncomfortable."

Pat: "I'm surprised to hear you say that, Frank. I really thought you were a team player. But hey, if supporting the team makes you uncomfortable, far be it from me to push."

Frank: "I'm sorry, I didn't mean to come off as harsh or uncaring. You know I care about the team."

Pat: "Hey, calm down. I'm just trying to make some sense of this whole bonus thing and to make sure our people didn't get robbed."

Frank: "Well, I guess if everyone else is sharing it's OK for me to tell you that my people got three and half percent. But please, can we keep that between us? We were told not to talk about the bonuses, and I don't feel great having disclosed this to you."

Pat: "No problem, Pat. I knew you were a team player. And no worries; this conversation is just between me and you. (Pat promptly runs off to spread the news that Frank broke the request for confidentiality and shared that his team got a three and a half percent bonus.)

Frank caved the minute Pat made him feel like he was being a bad person for trying to say "No." You'll notice that Pat didn't disclose what bonus his team got. Pat saw an opening to get what he wanted, and he grabbed it. This situation probably won't play out well for Frank, all because he lacked the ability to affirmatively say "No."

Example #2 (Good): Frank says "No" to an Advantage-Taker.

Pat: "I think my team got shortchanged on the annual bonus. What did your people get?"

Frank: "You know that we're not supposed to discuss the bonuses."

Pat: "That doesn't mean anything. They just say that to us because HR makes them. Everyone is talking about the bonuses. I just heard Carol say that her people got seven percent! I think that's outrageous, don't you? We both know that our teams work twice as hard as Carol's. So, what did your employees get?"

Frank: "It's apparent that you really want these numbers, Pat. However, my answer is no. We were both explicitly told not to share these numbers and I'm going to abide by that. I won't share the numbers."

Pat: "Hey, calm down. I thought you were a team player, but obviously I was wrong. I'm just trying to make some sense of this whole bonus thing and to make sure our people didn't get robbed. But if you don't want to share the numbers with me, that's cool."

Frank: "Again, it's clear that you really want these numbers, Pat. But my answer is still no."

Pat: "OK. I hear you." (Pat walks away, defeated).

In this example, Frank's response to Pat works because it's neither passive nor aggressive; instead, it's appropriately assertive. Advantage-Takers know that it's a waste of time to persist where no opportunity exists. And if they do still try to break you, just repeat your "No" and your original reason for declining, as Frank does in Example #2.

Once you've prepared your "No," you can relax because it's incredibly tough to defeat this strategy. It is a good idea when you're first getting the hang of it to script yourself and to practice. But soon enough, you'll be firmly, but nicely, asserting yourself with any anyone who tries to take advantage of you.

CHAPTER 8

THE CONFIDENTLY INCOMPETENT

Have you ever dealt with someone whose performance stinks, and they're not only clueless that their performance stinks but they're confident that their performance is good or even great? If you've worked with one or more of these Confidently Incompetent people, you likely experienced the Dunning-Kruger Effect in action.

Coined in 1999 by then-Cornell psychologists David Dunning and Justin Kruger, the eponymous Dunning-Kruger Effect is a cognitive bias whereby people who are incompetent at something are unable to recognize their own incompetence.[xii] Dunning and Kruger suggest that this phenomenon stems from what they refer to as a "dual burden." Not only are these people incompetent, but their incompetence robs them of the cognitive ability to realize just how inept they are.

The Confidently Incompetent person:

- Overestimates their own skill levels.
- Does not recognize the real skills and ability of other people.
- Does not recognize their own mistakes and lack of skill.

At work, Confidently Incompetent employees strongly believe that they're doing a great job (and will typically tell everyone about the great job they're doing), but they're actually doing a lousy job. Among the workplace problems this creates are poor performance, inability to receive constructive criticism, lack of professional growth (these people already think they're the best), and unhappy and disengaged coworkers who feel forced to pick up the slack from someone who frustratingly refuses to see how grossly incompetent they are.

The irony of the Dunning-Kruger Effect is that, as Professor Dunning notes, "The knowledge and intelligence that are required to be good at a task are often the same qualities needed to recognize that one is not good at that task—and if one lacks such knowledge and intelligence, one remains ignorant that one is not good at that task."[xiii]

The 1999 paper that launched the Dunning-Kruger Effect was titled "Unskilled and Unaware of It: How Difficulties in Recognizing One's Own Incompetence Lead to Inflated Self-Assessments."[xiv] Across four studies, Professor Dunning and his team administered tests of humor, grammar, and logic, and they found that participants scoring in the bottom quartile grossly overestimated their test performance and ability.

For example, in one of the studies, Cornell undergrads took a 20-item grammar test. After completing the test, the students estimated how their ability to "identify grammatically correct standard English" compared with others. And as you might expect, the lowest scoring students grossly overestimated their abilities. Those who scored at the 10th percentile (i.e. they scored higher than only 10% of others) rated their grammar abilities at the 67th percentile. In essence, their actual grammar ability was really poor, but they thought they were in the top third of people.

And it's not just college kids; you can find examples of the Dunning-Kruger Effect everywhere. One study of high-tech firms discovered that 32% to 42% of software engineers rated their skills as being in the top 5% of their companies. A nationwide survey found that 21% of Americans believe that it's 'very likely' or 'fairly likely' that they'll become millionaires within the next ten years. Drivers consistently rate themselves above average. Medical technicians overestimate their knowledge in real-world lab procedures.

Interestingly, professionals typically rate their performance significantly higher than their bosses do. In one meta-analysis involving more than 35,000 people, researchers found minimal correlation (.22) between people's self-rating on performance appraisals and the rating their boss gave them.[xv] That means there's not much relationship between the inflated ways we see ourselves and how our boss sees us. This helps explain all the incompetent, low-performing employees who, much to their managers' astonishment, demand better pay, perks, and promotions.

We also know from the more than 10,000 people who've taken Leadership IQ's online test "How Do You React To Constructive Criticism?"[xvi] that only 39% of employees handle constructive criticism by systematically dissecting every step leading up to the thing they just got criticized for. These 39% of people don't freak out or fight the feedback, instead, they want to understand and correct the underlying issues.

Now, it's not guaranteed that the other 61% are ensconced in Dunning-Kruger, but it is concerning that Dunning-Kruger may affect how some of these people receive critical feedback.

The Confidently Incompetent person may be employing a type of defensiveness that Professor Dunning and his colleagues call "expedient escape." This is where people find the most expedient avenue available to reject the feedback. For example, a Confidently Incompetent person might question the accuracy of the feedback (e.g. "You can't rate my emotional intelligence low just because I didn't smile enough in the staff meeting") or they might challenge the relevance of the feedback (e.g. "Emotional intelligence is not relevant to being a great financial analyst"). Either way, as Professor Dunning affirms, you're telling these difficult personalities things that may cause them to question what they believe and there's a good chance they won't take it very well.

For example, let's take the study in which David Dunning and his colleagues discovered that MBA students greatly overestimate their emotional intelligence.[xvii]

First, the researcher asked the students to rate how they thought they compared to American adults in general, and then they took an actual test of emotional intelligence. When Dunning's team looked at the worst performers, they found that students whose actual tests showed them at the 10th percentile (i.e. they only scored higher than 10% of American adults) had actually thought that their emotional intelligence was going to be around the 72nd percentile. In classic Dunning-Kruger fashion, the worst performers thought they were great and overestimated their emotional intelligence by 62 percentile points!

When these Dunning-Kruger sufferers were then given feedback about their poor results on the emotional intelligence test, they saw the test as less accurate and relevant than those who scored well on the test. They didn't like the results of the test, so their expedient escape reaction was that the test must be inaccurate and/or irrelevant.

Managing The Confidently Incompetent

It's a tough sell to get Confidently Incompetent employees to wake up to reality, but it's by no means a hopeless endeavor. When I spoke with Professor Dunning, he told me that the underperformance problem found in many organizations is often because these employees don't know that they could be doing better or what really great performance looks like. It's not that they're necessarily being defensive, rather they just lack the knowledge.

Professor Dunning said that research subjects were willing to criticize their own previous poor skills once they were trained up and could see the difference between their previous poor performance and their new improved performance. Unfortunately, one of my studies found that only 29% of employees say they 'Always' know whether their performance is where it should be. Meanwhile, a whopping 36% say they 'Never' or 'Rarely' know.[xviii] It's no wonder so many people suffer from Dunning-Kruger when most employees haven't gotten the feedback they need to know if they're doing a good or bad job.

Overcoming the Dunning-Kruger Effect starts by using the Confidently Incompetent Script to help Confidently Incompetent employees to think through how excellence is defined on the specific issue (e.g. behavior, attitude, etc.) on which we want them to improve. Once they have an idea of what excellence looks like, we're next going to make them think through how they would correct their performance if they were falling short of excellence. Finally, we're going to ask them to evaluate how they think their current performance stacks up to that definition of excellence.

Here's how the Confidently Incompetent Script works.

Confidently Incompetent Script

Step 1: Pick the area where the Confidently Incompetent employee needs to improve (e.g. behavior, attitude, etc.) and then ask them to describe what excellence looks like for that behavior, attitude, etc. For example, you might ask ***"What skills does it take to be a top financial analyst here?"*** or ***"If we look at the financial analysts who enjoy the greatest success at this firm, what kinds of technical and people skills do they have?"***

The goal here is to get the Confidently Incompetent person to think through the difference between bad, good and excellent work on this topic. If we start this conversation by telling them how bad their work is, they will immediately start looking for expedient escape routes (where people find the most expedient avenue they can to reject the feedback). If they struggle to come up with a sufficiently robust definition of excellence, we'll have to guide them in creating a better definition. Using phrases like "what about..." and "what else..." will be useful here.

Step 2: Once the Confidently Incompetent person has described what excellence looks like, ask them *"If you discovered that your performance on one of those attributes was lacking, what are some steps you might take to correct that?"*
Once the Confidently Incompetent person understands the difference between bad and excellent work, then we can start helping them to recognize that they may not be doing excellent work.

Step 3: Ask the Confidently Incompetent person to evaluate their own performance and whether it's meeting the definition of excellence. For example, we might *ask* ***"When you consider your recent work on this issue, especially in light of how we just defined excellence, how would you rate your skills?"***

One of a manager's biggest jobs in getting a Confidently Incompetent person to alter their behavior is ensuring that there are no expedient escape routes. If we deliver a criticism-laced tirade to an unwilling employee, we're just begging them to resist, devalue, or otherwise reject the feedback.

Remember that lots of people have no idea that their performance is subpar (aka the Dunning-Kruger effect). Ideally, we want to help Confidently Incompetent employees to criticize their own work and come to their own conclusions that their work is falling short of excellent.

The Confidently Incompetent Script in Action

Imagine a scenario where Pat is a financial analyst at a large company. Pat is absolutely convinced that he's great at doing his job, but the truth is that he is lacking in many areas including his interpersonal and communication skills, knowledge of the necessary software, and even his analytical abilities are weak.

Let's look at two examples where the boss tries to give Pat constructive feedback. In the first (bad) example, the boss launches right into the critical feedback and Pat immediately finds an expedient escape.

In the second (good) example, the boss closes off any expedient escape routes by first engaging Pat with a series of questions.

Example #1 (Bad): The boss launches right into the critical feedback and Pat immediately finds an expedient escape.

Boss: "Hey Pat, do you have a minute?"

Pat: "Sure, what's up?"

Boss: "I wanted to check in and see how things are going."

Pat: "Things are going great. You don't need to waste your time checking in with me. I've got everything under control."

Boss: "I thought I heard about some holdbacks on the project you and Ken are pulling together."

Pat: "I don't know what Ken might have told you, but the project is going great. I have everything under control. Maybe Ken is the one you should be talking to."

Boss: "OK, but maybe you could focus some more on Ken's ideas. It's often the case that you are so sure of yourself that it makes you unable or even unwilling to listen to anyone else's input and I think doing so would benefit you. This is a talented team and there's plenty of room for star performers."

Pat: "I'm the best financial analyst you've got, and I've got the highest success track record on the team to prove it. I don't know where this is coming from, but it's far more likely that Ken would benefit from listening more to me."

Boss: "Look, Pat, we've been here before. We've talked numerous times about the importance of emotional intelligence and how important it is to teamwork. I really need to see some changes in you. Can we talk about some of the reasons why you're so resistant to accepting this?"

Pat: "Oh Puh-leez! How do you even measure emotional intelligence? You can't rate my emotional intelligence low just because I didn't smile enough in the staff meeting or because Ken, or whoever, can't keep up with me. And even if emotional intelligence was a real concept, and I did rate low, it's not even relevant to the job and I'm the best you've got!"

This is an example of the Dunning-Kruger Effect, a cognitive bias whereby people who are incompetent at something are both unable to recognize their own incompetence and likely to feel confident that they actually are competent.

Here, Pat is employing a type of defensiveness called expedient escape where he finds the most expedient avenue he can to reject the feedback. This is why he challenges the accuracy of the feedback (e.g. "you can't rate my emotional intelligence low because I didn't smile enough in the staff meeting") and challenges the relevance of the feedback (e.g. "emotional intelligence is not relevant to the job"). If Pat saw his deficiencies, he wouldn't fight constructive criticism of his abilities and he wouldn't be so frustrating to deal with.

Example #2 (Good): The boss uses the Confidently Incompetent Script to close off any expedient escape routes.

Boss: "Pat, how are things going for you and Ken on that project?"

Pat: "Great. I've implemented some new data charts that I know will make the client happy. I've got a few other great ideas I'm working on as well."

Boss: "The new data charts sound good and I look forward to reviewing them. As I mentioned to the team this morning, I'm creating some definitions for what it takes to achieve excellent performance, and I want to meet individually with everyone to discuss this. Does that sound OK to you?"

Pat: "Yeah, sure. I know all about top performance, so how can I help?"

Boss: "For starters, if we look at the financial analysts who truly achieve excellence and enjoy the greatest success at this firm, what kinds of technical and people skills do they have?"

Pat: "I speak from years of experience when I say it takes attention to detail, accuracy and a highly developed sense of discretion and confidentiality."

Boss: "What about people skills?"

Pat: "Well, you've got to be able to tell the story behind the numbers. I put a lot of work into doing that for the talking points I presented in this morning's meeting, for example."

Boss: "What about people skills within your own team?"

Pat: "We deal with numbers and data; it's not exactly warm and fuzzy stuff."

Boss: "When you work within the team, what does it take to truly achieve excellence?"

Pat: "Well, it helps when people actually listen to my ideas and respond to what I'm saying. Nothing is more frustrating than when I'm ignored. I've had some really good ideas on how to build on what others are doing, but I can't tell you how many times I've been rebuffed when I start to speak."

Boss: "Let me make sure I have that right. So you're saying that the excellent performers in this company are the people who listen to and consider the ideas of others. And it sounds like poor performance would be ignoring or even belittling someone else's ideas. Is that correct?"

Pat: "Exactly, and you know what, you can take it up a notch and add in considering other people's ideas, working to support those ideas, and getting other people to buy in and support those ideas."

Boss: "OK, so then when I'm defining excellence, I am going to add 'I listen to ideas of my teammates and I work to get others to accept and support their good ideas.' Is that correct?"

Pat: "Yes. Just this morning, for example, when I was working with Ken, I could tell he was tuning me out. It's the most frustrating thing."

Boss: "If you discovered that your performance on that attribute was lacking, what are some steps you might take to correct that?"

Pat: "I've read that one of the big rules of listening is to take in the entire message, no interruptions allowed, and to suspend interpretations. You know, to go in with an open mind that someone might know something you don't."

Boss: "When you consider your recent work with Ken, especially in light of how we just defined excellence, how would you rate your listening skills regarding hearing his good ideas?"

Pat: "Honestly, I don't think he's had any good ideas. Basically, I've been steering the project."

Boss: "When I spoke to Ken earlier today, he told me a few of the ideas that he said he's shared with you. But when I just asked you how the project was progressing, you told me about your idea for the data charts but nothing about Ken's ideas. Why do you think that is?"

Pat: "I have no idea. As far as I know I've been listening to what Ken has to say. My listening skills are excellent. I'm the best listener on the team."

Boss: "I want to go back to how we just defined excellence. You said that one aspect was 'listening to ideas of my teammates' and another was 'to go in with an open mind that someone might know something you don't.' Now, if you can't name one single idea that Ken has had, are you really meeting your own definition of excellence?"

Pat: "I guess I'm not."

Boss: "I really like your definition of excellence. Can you see why I think it's so good for all of us to achieve that level of performance?"

Pat: "I guess I need to focus more on hitting my own standards."

Boss: "Would you be open to calling Ken into this meeting so the three of us can discuss the ideas you both have for this project? It would be a great opportunity for all of us to practice our good listening skills."

Pat: "Sure. I can do that."

The boss engages Pat with a series of questions that guide him into being accountable for the behaviors that he himself has just described. With no available expedient escape, Pat has no choice but to take the meeting with Ken and to live up to the high performer behaviors he has just described.

CHAPTER 9

NARCISSISTS

Narcissists are those people who have an exaggerated sense of self-importance that presents in wanting excessive admiration. The drivers behind these their exaggerated sense of self-importance include envy, a fragile sense of self, and sometimes even paranoia.

Narcissists typically do whatever it takes to meet their own needs, regardless of the expense to others. This makes them an obstructive force to the whole team. To complicate things even more, Narcissists are usually reasonably bright, and sometimes incredibly so. They tend to be perfectionists, they suffer from paranoia, and they typically become insecure when they don't receive the adoration that they feel they're entitled to.

Ohio State researchers have recently found that if you want to learn if someone is a Narcissist, all you have to do is ask them to what extent they agree with the statement "I am a narcissist." Across 11 experiments, involving more than 2,200 people, the researchers could reliably identify narcissistic people just by asking them that question, rated on a scale ranging from 1 (not very true of me) to 7 (very true of me).[xix] "People who are narcissists are almost proud of the fact. You can ask them directly because they don't see narcissism as a negative quality—they believe they are superior to other people and are fine with saying that publicly," said Brad Bushman, co-author of the study and a professor of communication and psychology at Ohio State University.[xx]

Narcissists are incredibly tough to manage, especially if you try to tackle their narcissism directly. Narcissists don't generally see narcissism as a problem, so if you try to correct their narcissistic attitude, you're likely to meet massive resistance or dismissiveness. That's why if you read much of 'managing narcissists' literature, the two most common recommendations are to avoid these difficult personalities altogether or to feign niceness until you can get away from them.

That's the bad news. But there is a bright spot here; Narcissists typically have other difficult personalities coexisting with their narcissism. For example, many Narcissists are also Blamers, Negative Personalities or Dramatics who will use their blame, negativity and drama as a way of seeking attention and admiration. And it's those comorbid bad attitudes that give us a much easier place to start.

The reason why this chapter on Narcissists follows the chapters on Dramatics, Negative Personalities, Blamers, and the Confidently Incompetent is that if your Narcissist also has any of these difficult personality issues, start there first. In other words, make their narcissism the last aspect of their difficult personality that you address. Drama, blame, negativity, etc. are all significantly easier problems to manage, so use these as your starting point.

If there aren't comorbid difficult personalities, and all you've got to work with is their narcissism, then you can use the following approach.

Managing Narcissists

Managing Narcissists requires leveraging the paranoia, the envy, the insecurity and the perfectionism of these difficult personalities to lead them to better performance. We do this by using the following Narcissist Script which first requires finding something, even a small thing, that the Narcissist has done poorly or below their normal standards. If they make a mistake, as we all do, that's terrific for our purposes. Once you've got something that they've done that's wrong, or even subpar, you're going to use that as an opportunity to apply the script to curb their narcissism.

The script works by subtly co-opting the Narcissist's inflated ego with a compliment that appeals to their perfectionism and putative brilliance but also challenges and takes advantage of their insecurity by holding them to up to their own high standards.

Narcissist Script

Step 1: Compliment the Narcissist, but also supply a challenge. For example, *"I was surprised that with your brilliant track record that you'd expose yourself to attacks of sloppiness by not doing those really simple reports."*

We can't directly attack the Narcissist's arrogance, but we can take their narcissism and use it to our advantage. And we do this in Step 1 by complimenting them in a way that plays off their insecurity and perfectionism.

Typically, the only reason that narcissism is tolerated in the workplace is because these difficult personalities actually do good work (if they were narcissistic and incompetent, they would likely have been fired by now). So finding something that they've done that's a mistake, or even just below their normal standards, gives us an opportunity to curb their narcissism. When we compliment the Narcissist's previous track record, we're avoiding attacking them directly (and thus making them defensive and dismissive). But we're also taking advantage of their insecurities by creating a challenge (e.g. pointing out that other people will probably mock their sloppiness because they forgot to do something very simple).

Step 2: Appeal to their perfectionism and putative brilliance. For example, *"You know how people can focus on those little things and miss everything else because one mistake shakes their confidence in the entire body of work."*

In Step 2, we poke at the Narcissist's envy and paranoia a bit more directly by saying that this one little mistake could shake peoples' confidence in their abilities. We pointed out their mistake in Step 1, but that's often not enough to change a Narcissist's attitude, especially as they can be quick to dismiss errors, especially small ones. But when we tell them that this one mistake could have significant ramifications for how others see them, that's much more likely to get their attention, and thus deflate some of their narcissism.

Step 3: Take advantage of their paranoia. For example, *"This really seems like a missed opportunity for ______ (e.g. "showing off your skills in front of this audience")."*

In this third step, we're subtly bringing our comments back to their narcissism and pointing out that if they're seeking admiration (which Narcissists want), they really missed an opportunity here. The goal is not to undo their narcissism, because that's not realistic. Instead, we're after a slight deflating of their ego. And we accomplish this by very gently poking some holes in their fragile sense of self and leveraging their paranoia and insecurities.

Step 4: If your Narcissist has really become a problem for the team, and you feel like you need to push them a little harder

to cease their narcissism, then you can add the phrase, ***"And I can't have our team undermined because our supposedly brilliant _________ (example: report writer) is falling far short of perfection."***
Step 4 takes the script one step further should you feel like you need to take a harder line with the Narcissist. This final step makes it quite clear that you will not tolerate their narcissism.

Through this script, we're essentially leveraging the Narcissist's weaknesses to curb their narcissism. We're not attacking them directly, because that won't work on a Narcissist. But we're also not letting poor attitudes and behavior escape our notice. We're trying to get productivity out of them, while subtly deflating some of their narcissism. Note that if they're not productive and still wildly narcissistic, then this is a toxic personality and you'll need to jump to Chapter 10: "Talented Terrors."

The Narcissist Script in Action

Imagine a scenario where Pat, a Narcissist, has made several errors in completing an important client report.

Let's look at two examples where Pat's boss tries to deliver constructive feedback about the report. In the first (bad) example, the boss attacks Pat directly which results in resistance and dismissiveness.

In the second (good) example, the boss uses the Narcissist Script to subtly co-opt Pat's inflated ego with a compliment that also challenges and takes advantage of her insecurity by holding her up to her own high standards.

Example #1 (Bad): The boss attacks Pat directly.

Boss: "Pat, I need to talk to you about some problems with the ACME report."

Pat: "Problems? I doubt that. I checked that report thoroughly before submitting it. No one is as thorough as I am when it comes to writing reports."

Boss: "Actually the bubble charts are way off. I believe I asked you to work with Frank on those charts to make sure they were correct. Did you do that?"

Pat: "I really don't think I need Frank, or anyone else's help. You do recall that I'm a member of Mensa? My IQ is in the triple digits. If anything, Frank should be coming to me for help."

Boss: "I don't know about that, but I do know that the charts are incorrect, and the client rejected the report. It needs to be rewritten, by tomorrow, and I want you to work with Frank on getting those charts correct."

Pat: "Well, I'll certainly look at the report, but if there are any errors, it's not my fault. Maybe the client just doesn't know how to read the charts properly."

Boss: "That's enough, Pat. There are errors and you are the only one who worked on this report. No one else touched it, even though I specifically asked you to bring in Frank to help. Honestly, your narcissistic behavior is exhausting."

Pat: "Oh, so I'm a narcissist? Is that what you think? How about instead we just agree that I am the best person you've got on this team and you can't handle that. Maybe you're just afraid that I'm better than you are."

Boss: "That's not what's happening here, Pat. But I do need you to act like a member of this team if you wish to remain a member of this team. And that means working with Frank, or whomever, when I ask you to. There are no superstars in this department. We are a team, and it will serve you well to remember that."

Pat: "I see what you're doing. You're trying to bring me down to the level of everyone else, aren't you? Look, I hear things, and I know that you got passed up for that promotion you wanted last month. I'm sure you're unhappy about that but trying to take it out on me isn't cool. My record here is spotless, and I'm not going to let you ruin that."

Clearly, directly confronting Pat about her narcissism did not work out well for the boss.

Example #2 (Good): The boss uses the Narcissist Script to subtly co-opt Pat's inflated ego with a compliment that also challenges her and takes advantage of her insecurity by holding her up to her own high standards.

Boss: "Pat, the bubble charts on the ACME report were incorrect. I'm surprised that with your brilliant track record you'd expose yourself to attacks of sloppiness by not getting them right."

Pat: "I seriously doubt there are any errors. I checked that report thoroughly before submitting it. No one is as thorough as I am when it comes to writing reports."

Boss: "The charts are incorrect, and that's why I asked you to work with Frank on those charts; to make sure the work was double checked. ACME rejected the report and it needs to be rewritten and resubmitted tomorrow. I'm afraid that this error may have damaged the client relationship. You know how sloppy mistakes like this can cause people to lose confidence. Even your coworkers are feeling pretty shaken up about it. None of us want to lose the ACME account, and to lose it over such a preventable error would be extra bad."

Pat: "I'm sure ACME isn't going anywhere. I have a great track record with them. Whatever the problem is, it can't be that bad. I'll look at the report, but there's really no reason for me to work with Frank. I can handle this."

Boss: "Look, I'm not going to argue with you about working with Frank. But if those charts are incorrect again, we will likely lose the ACME account. Of course, if we get the charts right, and we make ACME happy, that's something everyone will be pleased about. All I know is that I can't have our team undermined because our supposedly brilliant report writer is falling short of perfection."

Pat: "Fine. I'll find Frank and we'll get the revised report to ACME first thing in the morning."

Here, the boss uses the Narcissist Script to subtly co-opt Pat's inflated ego with a compliment that also challenges and takes advantage of her insecurity by holding her up to her own high standards.

CHAPTER 10

TALENTED TERRORS

When correctly used, the techniques shared in the previous chapters will allow you to change most of the bad behaviors and troublesome attitudes that difficult personalities bring to the workplace. But every so often you will encounter a difficult personality who remains impervious to your attempts to manage them. And the reason why these people are generally unwilling to fix their bad attitude is that, for years, their fantastic technical skills have gotten them preferential treatment and glowing performance reviews.

We call these difficult personalities "Talented Terrors" because they have very high levels of technical skills and innate intelligence coupled with a terrible attitude. These low performers are like "emotional vampires." They won't actually suck your blood, but the frustration of dealing with them will suck the life out of you.

Talented Terrors are typically masterful at turning their problematic attitudes on and off as it serves them best, and they don't pick fights they can't win. For example, no matter how difficult they may act towards you on a given day, when the Chairman of the Board walks by their desk, it's all sunshine and buttercups. "Hello Sir, wonderful day we're having!" they might say. "You're looking more fit than ever. Have you lost weight? I just finished reading your letter to the shareholders, and it was brilliant as always, Sir!"

Of course, as soon as the Chairman leaves, the sunshine turns to dark and threatening clouds and the Talented Terror returns to sucking the life out of you with their bad attitude.

If the techniques from the earlier chapters have not allowed you to guide a difficult personality to significantly alter their problematic behaviors and attitudes, you're likely dealing with a Talented Terror.

Managing Talented Terrors

Managing Talented Terrors requires a few extra steps which you'll find outlined in the four-part Talented Terrors Script below. You might feel tempted to avoid dealing with your Talented Terrors. After all, while they are difficult to deal with attitudinally, they are highly skilled. But it's important to remember that your other employees, and your customers, are relying on you to do something about these low performers who are infecting your workplace with their bad attitudes. It's a false kindness to let the Talented Terror go on thinking they're a high performer because it's not going to help anyone if their behavior doesn't change.

Because we've exhausted the "nicer" scripts provided in the earlier chapters, it's time to sharpen our message to make it crystal clear to Talented Terrors that their bad attitudes and behaviors must stop. This doesn't mean being hostile or nasty, but it does require speaking factually, candidly and assertively.

The goal is to always speak objectively to Talented Terrors. For example, if we objectively say, "Company policy states that your responsibility is to fulfill your work commitments on time. However, I just went into a meeting with Client X without the information I needed because I didn't have your work," we're presenting the Talented Terror with only the unemotional facts. (Remember the **FIRE Model** from Chapter 1 where we learned to separate the **Facts** from the emotionally charged **Interpretations**, **Reactions** and desired **Ends**?) When we clearly present only the facts, it demands a level of culpability that even the most calculating of Talented Terrors will find difficult to deny.

An important part of speaking factually is to avoid using absolute language, for example, words like *always* and *never.* (My rule on absolutes is: It's Always a good idea to Never use words like "always" and "never.") Words like this are hyperbole and they often appear in exaggerated statements or claims that draw the emphasis away from the facts. No one is *always* or *never* anything. Are you '*always* on time' or '*never* wrong'? Probably not, and neither are your Talented Terrors.

Accusing a Talented Terror of something by using absolute language, for example "you *always* show up late to meetings" or "you're *never* productive in meetings," is laying the groundwork for failed communication. These clever low performers will only fight off your accusations by dredging up the memory of some previous meeting when they arrived early or went above and beyond to produce great work. Make no mistake, the Talented Terror will find a way to contradict your absolute statement, and it will weaken your ability to effectively manage them.

Keeping your cool is important with all difficult personalities, including Talented Terrors. When you call a Talented Terror in to a meeting to discuss their bad attitude, you're likely going to be feeling some emotions; usually some form of anger or frustration. If you lose your cool, your argument is going to come off as overblown and lose impact. Staying calm during Talented Terror conversations may sound trivial or obvious, but it needs mentioning as these difficult personalities have a unique ability to get under a leader's skin.

Remember, Talented Terrors have had plenty of time to hone their bad behavior and they know how to wield it like a pro. This probably isn't the first time a boss has called them out on their bad attitude, and they're just waiting for you to get angry and speak without thinking. Because as soon as you say or do something illogical (e.g. using non-factual absolute language), they'll turn the situation around on you, and before you know it, you'll be apologizing to them.

Don't be a victim of your own emotions. Pay attention to the triggers that provoke you and set you off emotionally and respect those triggers. That way, when you see a trigger coming your way, you can more easily dodge that bullet and keep your cool. For example, if you know that you're easily led to anger when you're tired, don't try to carry out a tough conversation with a Talented Terror (or any difficult personality) after a poor night's sleep. Or, if you get cranky and lose your patience when you're hungry, don't hold an important meeting until after you eat something.

I recommend the **HALT** approach when managing Talented Terrors as an easy and effective method of keeping anger and other unproductive emotions at bay. If you're **Hungry**, **Angry**, **Lonely**, or **Tired** (all emotionally compromised positions), delay the conversation until your mood shifts or you can get some sleep or food. It's not like you're trying to step out on the discussion or avoid it, you're just rescheduling it for a better time.

Here's the four-part script to follow for managing Talented Terrors.

Talented Terror Script

Step 1: Get right to the point by saying, *"I've called you in today because there's a problem with your recent performance."*
In many of the earlier scripts we took a gentler approach to opening the conversation. But because this Talented Terror has resisted those entreaties, we need to show them that this conversation will be very different.

Step 2: Describe the behavior or attitude that needs to change using factual, unemotional and specific language. For example, *"In Tuesday's task force meeting, you made three biting and sarcastic remarks during our brainstorming session."*

Step 3: Clearly explain that this attitude/behavior is not acceptable and cannot be allowed to continue. For example, *"That is not acceptable behavior in that setting and it will not be allowed to continue."*

Step 4: State that you believe they're capable of change but that only they can make the choice to do so. This can go as follows:

"Now, I can't force you to change, and I won't try. But what I will say is that you have a choice. You can change your behavior or keep it where it is. If you change, you will be much more effective, and I think you'll see your teammates respond more positively. If you decide to change, I can work with you to outline a very specific action plan with clear expectations.

If you opt not to change, then we'll begin an improvement plan which, without significant progress, could ultimately result in termination. (Insert your own HR policies here.) I believe you can change this behavior. But only you can choose the path that's right for you. Just be clear that there are only two options here and maintaining your present course is not one of them. You can give me your decision right now or you can take 24 hours to make a decision."

It's important to always give Talented Terrors a choice. Leadership grants you a certain level of authority, but that doesn't mean you can force people to do something against their will. If you try and box the Talented Terror into a corner, their behavior will just get worse. They'll become defensive and assume an attacking position that makes it even more difficult to reach the resolve you want.

Your goal here is to eradicate the behaviors associated with the bad attitude and that means outlining the choices and enforcing the consequences. After that, it's up to your Talented Terrors whether they decide to walk away, to continue with their bad behaviors and face the outlined negative consequences, or to change their behavior and enjoy the reward of positive consequences. The choice may be up to them, but you still control how long they have to make that choice.

After you lay out the facts and outline the consequences, offer your Talented Terrors the choice of taking 24 hours to think things over. You've likely given them a lot to take in, and they alone bear burden of deciding how they will respond. By giving them some time to think it over, they're going to make a smarter decision; one they are more likely to abide by.

The Talented Terror Script in Action

Imagine a scenario where Pat is the manager of a retail store. One of his employees, Frank, knows the products better than anyone, but he also has a lousy attitude. For example. Frank is confrontational with coworkers and has often been overhead making negative comments about the company to customers.

Because of Frank's skilled product knowledge, Pat has historically tolerated his lousy attitude. But an overwhelming number of recent customer and coworker complaints about Frank have made it clear that Frank's bad attitude is hurting the organization far more than his skills are helping it. For the past three months, Pat has kept a written ledger of Frank's attitudinal problems; jotting each one down as it happens, and he now feels fully prepared to confront Frank about his bad attitude.

Let's look at two examples (bad and good) of Pat talking to Frank. In the first (bad) example, Pat allows himself to get angry with Frank, thereby giving Frank control of the conversation.

In the second (good) example, Pat uses the Talented Terror Script to keep his cool and effectively give Frank a clear choice of "improve" or "remove."

Example #1 (Bad): Pat gets angry with Frank and gives Frank control of the conversation.

Pat: "Thanks for coming in today, Frank. It's come to my attention that you've got some attitudinal issues that are negatively affecting some of your coworkers and our customers. I've compiled a list of these issues as I've observed them over the past few months. I'd like for us to review this list together and discuss what can be done because I strongly believe these issues are holding you back from your best performance."

[Pat starts reading from his written ledger of Frank's attitudinal problems. But as he reads through the list, his anger builds as he realizes just how many times Frank's bad attitude has harmed the organization. In an effort to keep his cool, Pat quickly changes his tactic.]

Pat: "Look, I could go on reading this list, but the point here is that your attitude is lousy. You represent the company in a negative light to customers, you criticize your coworkers, and you have no respect for the authority I hold as manager. Your bad attitude is weighing heavily on this organization, and I need it to stop at once."

Frank: "I'm curious why none of this comes up when you need my expertise. Like last week when only I had the experience and knowledge to help that customer who had all the product questions? And how about the time I helped Andy over in housewares when the wrong shipment came in? If you recall, I was the only one who volunteered to stay late to help sort out that mess. And how about when you asked me to help in electronics during the holidays? I got right to work without any argument, even though it isn't even my department. So how can you say I'm negative to customers and coworkers and that I don't respect your leadership?"

Pat just learned the hard way that you can't let an employee's attitudinal problems build up over time and then expect to drop the hammer on it and fix the behavior in a single, emotionally charged conversation. Talented Terrors are smart, and they stockpile every positive performance example they can, so they are ready to fight back when they are called to task.

Pat's focus may be on Frank's bad attitude with his ledger of wrongs, but Frank is way ahead of him with his own list of all the things he's done right. This weakens Pat's argument by making it look overblown and irrational. And while Pat's accumulated irritation is finally reaching its peak, Frank is feeling calm and in control as he savors every moment of watching Pat's frustration explode.

Example #2 (Good): Pat uses the Talented Terror Script to give Frank a clear choice of "improve" or "remove."

Pat: "Frank, I've called you in today because there's a problem with your recent performance. In the past two weeks, I've witnessed five customer interactions where I've heard you expressing negative comments about the company to customers. That's just not acceptable behavior for that setting and it won't be allowed to continue.

Now, I can't force you to change, and I won't try. You have a choice: you can change your behavior or keep it where it is. If you change, you will be much more effective, and I think you'll see your teammates respond more positively. If you decide to change, I can work with you to outline a very specific action plan with clear expectations. If you opt not to change, then we'll begin an improvement plan which, without significant progress, could ultimately result in termination. (Insert your own HR policies here.)

I believe you can change this behavior, Frank, but only you can choose the path that's right for you. Just be clear that there are only two options here, and maintaining your present course is not one of them. You can give me your decision right now, or you can take 24 hours to make a decision."

How to Deal with the Talented Terror's Response

After you deliver the Talented Terror Script, there are several ways in which these difficult personalities might respond. A perfect response would be acceptance. For instance, Frank would say, "You're absolutely correct and I want to get back on track right away." Typically, when you the deliver the Talented Terror Script correctly it will go one of two ways. You're either going to get acceptance or the complete opposite: where the employee states an unwillingness to play by the rules and expresses a desire to just get out.

But sometimes you'll get a slightly different response, for example:

- Denial: "But I didn't do anything wrong."
- Narcissism: "You can't come down on me like this; I'm the best person you've got!"
- Anger: "How dare you insult me like this."
- Blame: "Bob's the one you should be talking to; he's the one who always messes up."
- Drama: (includes tears or other forms of histrionics).

Regardless of the response you get, there's a simple technique that will keep the conversation on track. It's what psychologists call the Broken Record Technique, and it works just like it sounds: "I hear you, now let me repeat, (Insert Talented Terror Script here)." And you walk the employee through the whole script again.

The Broken Record Technique works if you stick to the script and don't indulge whatever defense the Talented Terror is offering up. Talented Terrors may be low performers, but they're not stupid. They are much better at having a bad attitude than you are at managing them, and that includes their talent for manipulating the conversation, so it turns in their favor.

Your best chance at keeping the communication on track is to stick to the script with the Broken Record Technique. You may have to repeat the script two or three times, but after that, it's time to say, "Okay, I've made my point. This conversation is over."

Repeating yourself with the Broken Record Technique may feel a bit awkward at first. But keep in mind that good management is by and large a performing art, and just like any performer, you need to practice. If you have teenagers, they typically love to play the role of Talented Terror and make wonderful practice partners. They'll give you every form of bad attitude and drama you can think of, and that will force you to get comfortable with calmly repeating yourself.

If the Talented Terror Agrees to Make a Change

If a Talented Terror agrees to make a change for the better, you need to get them started towards redemption right away. This includes explaining exactly what it will take to meet expectations and how you will be measuring improvement. Giving Talented Terrors a clear and specific breakdown of what 'bad', 'good' and 'excellent' behavior looks and sounds like gives them a definitive guide by which they can judge for themselves whether they are on track.

CHAPTER 11

CONCLUSION

As I said in the Introduction, managing difficult personalities is never fun. Most difficult personalities have had years of practice at behaving badly and very few of them have any desire to change. That's why it takes a targeted, scientific approach to make an impact.

And we do need to make an impact. Difficult personalities aren't just annoying, frustrating and exhausting; in many cases they directly diminish (and even destroy) business value because they wield real power over other team members. And when those other team members find difficult personalities intimidating, demoralizing and fatiguing, you're going to see higher turnover, lost productivity, breakdowns and miscommunication, and much more.

But here's the good news: You've got this. Managing difficult personalities is like any other skill in that good techniques plus practice equals great results. And if you're willing to fully implement the techniques in this book, I know you're going to see significant results!

In addition to the scripts in this book, go to www.leadershipiq.com and download your cheat sheets so that whenever you encounter a difficult personality, you've got a quick refresher at your fingertips.

ABOUT THE AUTHOR

Mark Murphy is a *New York Times* bestselling author, contributor to *Forbes* and *CNBC*, and founder of Leadership IQ, a research and training firm.

Mark is ranked as one of the Top 30 leadership gurus in the world, and some of his most well-known research studies include "Are SMART Goals Dumb?," "Why CEOs Get Fired," "Why New Hires Fail," "High Performers Can Be Less Engaged," and "Don't Expect Layoff Survivors to Be Grateful."

Mark leads one of the world's largest databases of original leadership research, and his work has appeared in the *Wall Street Journal*, the *New York Times*, *Fortune*, *Forbes*, *Bloomberg Businessweek*, and *U.S. News & World Report*. Mark has also appeared on CNN, NPR, CBS *Sunday Morning*, ABC's *20/20*, and the Fox Business Network.

Mark has lectured at the United Nations, Harvard Business School, the Clinton Foundation, Microsoft, Merck, MasterCard, Charles Schwab, Aflac, and hundreds more.

Mark's most recent books include *Leadership Styles: How to Discover and Leverage Yours* and *Truth At Work: The Science of Delivering Tough Messages*. He is the author of the *New York Times* bestseller *Hundred Percenters: Challenge Your People to Give It Their All and They'll Give You Even More.* Before that, his book *Hiring for Attitude* was featured in *Fast Company* and the *Wall Street Journal* and was chosen as a top business book by CNBC.

Some of his other books include *HARD Goals: The Science of Getting from Where You Are to Where You Want to Be* and *The Deadly Sins of Employee Retention.*

FOR MORE INFORMATION

For free downloadable resources including quizzes and discussion guides, please visit www.leadershipiq.com

ENDNOTES

i Murphy, Mark (2018). *Interruptions At Work Are Killing Your Productivity*. Retrieved from https://www.leadershipiq.com/blogs/leadershipiq/interruptions-at-work-are-killing-your-productivity.

ii Murphy, Mark (2017). *How Many Hours Leaders Need To Spend With Their Employees*. Retrieved from https://www.leadershipiq.com/blogs/leadershipiq/35352257-all-great-leadership-styles-begin-by-spending-time-with-employees

iii Murphy, Mark (2016). Low Performers May Be More Engaged Than High Performers. Retrieved from https://www.leadershipiq.com/blogs/leadershipiq/35354881-employee-engagement-shocker-low-performers-may-be-more-engaged-than-high-performers

iv Murphy, Mark (2015). *Why CEOs Get Fired*. Retrieved from https://www.leadershipiq.com/blogs/leadershipiq/35353153-why-the-ceo-gets-fired-change-management-and-more

v Newman, D., Joseph, D., & MacCann, C. (2010). Emotional Intelligence and Job Performance: The Importance of Emotion Regulation and Emotional Labor Context. *Industrial and Organizational Psychology, 3*(2), 159-164. doi:10.1111/j.1754-9434.2010.01218.x

vi Murphy, Mark. (2015). Why New Hires Fail. Retrieved from https://www.leadershipiq.com/blogs/leadershipiq/35354241-why-new-hires-fail-emotional-intelligence-vs-skills

vii Berger, Jonah A. and Milkman, Katherine L. (December 25, 2009). *What Makes Online Content Viral?* Retrieved from https://ssrn.com/abstract=1528077

viii Murphy, Mark (2018) *Fake News Hits The Workplace.* Retrieved from https://www.leadershipiq.com/blogs/leadershipiq/study-fake-news-hits-the-workplace

ix Fast, N. J., & Tiedens, L. Z. (2010). Blame contagion: The automatic transmission of self-serving attributions. *Journal of Experimental Social Psychology, 46*(1), 97-106. dx.doi.org/10.1016/j.jesp.2009.10.007

x Murphy, Mark (2017). *The Risks Of Ignoring Employee Feedback.* Retrieved from https://www.leadershipiq.com/blogs/leadershipiq/study-the-risks-of-ignoring-employee-feedback.

xi Murphy, Mark (2015). *Building Trust In The Workplace.* Retrieved from https://www.leadershipiq.com/blogs/leadershipiq/study-the-risks-of-ignoring-employee-feedback.

xii Dunning, David. "The Dunning–Kruger Effect: On Being Ignorant of One's Own Ignorance." *Advances in Experimental Social Psychology*, 44:247–96. Elsevier, 2011.

xiii Murphy, Mark. (2018). *The Dunning-Kruger Effect Shows Why Some People Think They're Great Even When Their Work Is Terrible.* Retrieved from https://www.forbes.com/sites/markmurphy/2017/01/24/the-dunning-kruger-effect-shows-why-some-people-think-theyre-great-even-when-their-work-is-terrible/

xiv Kruger,Justin&Dunning,David. (2000). Unskilled and Unaware of It: How Difficulties in Recognizing One's Own Incompetence Lead to Inflated Self-Assessments. *Journal of Personality and Social Psychology*. 77. 1121-34. 10.1037//0022-3514.77.6.1121.

xv Harris, Michael & Schaubroeck, John. (2006). A meta-analysis of self-supervisor, self-peer, and peer-supervisor ratings. *Personnel Psychology*. 41. 43 - 62. 10.1111/j.1744-6570.1988.tb00631.x.

xvi Murphy, Mark (2017). *How Do You React To Constructive Criticism?* Quiz. Retrieved from https://www.leadershipiq.com/blogs/leadershipiq/41783745-quiz-how-do-you-react-to-constructive-criticism

xvii *The Journal of Applied Psychology*. 2014 Jan;99(1):125-37. doi: 10.1037/a0034138. Epub 2013 Aug 19.

xviii Murphy, Mark (2016). *Fewer Than Half Of Employees Know If They're Doing A Good Job.* Retrieved from https://www.forbes.com/sites/markmurphy/2016/09/04/fewer-than-half-of-employees-know-if-theyre-doing-a-good-job/

xix Konrath S, Meier BP, Bushman BJ (2014) Development and Validation of the Single Item Narcissism Scale (SINS). *PLoS ONE* 9(8): e103469. https://doi.org/10.1371/journal.pone.0103469

xx Ohio State University (2014). *Just one simple question can identify narcissistic people.* Retrieved from www.sciencedaily.com/releases/2014/08/140805150645.htm

Made in the USA
Columbia, SC
15 January 2024